To Kay & Chuck

Christmas 1992

Love, Harriet

A Most Surprising Song

EXPLORING
THE
MYSTICAL EXPERIENCE

By
Louann Stahl

Unity Books
Unity Village, MO 64065 U.S.A.

Text and cover designed by Chad Pio

Cover was created by combining globe photograph
by Rick Fischer/Masterfile with staff photography.

Copyright © 1992 by Louann Stahl
All Rights Reserved
LLC 91-065820
ISBN 0-87159-106-5
Canada GST R132529033

 This book is printed on recycled paper.

Dedication

FOR MY FATHER WHO GAVE ME THE SPIRITUAL DIRECTION, FOR MY MOTHER WHO GAVE ME THE COURAGE, FOR MY HUSBAND WHO GAVE ME THE ENCOURAGEMENT AND SUPPORT THAT MADE THIS WORK POSSIBLE.

Acknowledgments

I give my thanks and appreciation to my readers, to Jason Petosa for his astute editing, to Joan Putthoff for her unswerving enthusiasm, and also to Maggie Wagner, my editor at Unity Books, for her help and dedication. And, of course, to all the mystics quoted herein who really wrote the book.

Table of Contents

The author gratefully acknowledges permission to reprint from the following sources:

Autobiography of a Yogi by Paramahansa Yogananda. Copyright © 1946 by Paramahansa Yogananda, renewed 1974 by Self-Realization Fellowship. Copyright © 1981 Self-Realization Fellowship. All rights reserved. Reprinted with permission.

The Axis and the Rim by Arthur W. Osborn. Copyright © 1967 by Arthur W. Osborn. Reprinted by permission of Theosophical Publishing House, Wheaton, Illinois.

The Collected Poems and Plays of Rabindranath Tagore. (New York: Macmillan, 1937) Reprinted by permission of Macmillan Publishing Company.

A Course in Miracles. Copyright © 1975. Reprinted by permission of Foundation for Inner Peace, Inc.

Do You See What I See? by Jae Jah Noh. Copyright © 1977 by Edwin Smith. Reprinted by permission of Theosophical Publishing House, Wheaton, Illinois.

Ecstasy: A Way of Knowing by Andrew M. Greeley. Copyright © 1974, reprinted by permission of publisher, Prentice-Hall, Inc., Englewood Cliffs, New Jersey.

Ecstatic Confessions by Martin Buber. Copyright © English translation 1985 by Harper & Row, Publishers, Inc. Reprinted by permission of HarperCollins Publishers, Inc.

The Enlightened Society by John L. Hill. Copyright © 1987 by John Hill. Reprinted by permission of Theosophical Publishing House, Wheaton, Illinois.

The Essential Unity of All Religions by Bhagavan Das. First edition, 1932. Reprinted by permission of Theosophical Publishing House, Wheaton, Illinois.

The Expansion of Awareness by Arthur W. Osborn. Copyright © 1961 by Theosophical Publishing House. Reprinted by permission of Theosophical Publishing House, Wheaton, Illinois.

The Experience of No-Self by Bernadette Roberts. Copyright © 1982. Reprinted by arrangement with Shambhala Publications, Inc., 300 Massachusetts Ave., Boston, Massachusetts 02115.

In Search of Identity by Anwar Sadat. Copyright © 1977, 1978 by the Village of Mit-Abul-Kum, English translation © 1977, 1978 by Harper & Row, Publishers, Inc. Reprinted by permission of HarperCollins Publishers, Inc.

The Invisible Writing by Arthur Koestler. Copyright © 1954, 1969 by Arthur Koestler. Reprinted by permission of Peters Fraser & Dunlop Ltd., London.

The Kabir Book by Robert Bly. Copyright © 1971, 1977 by Robert Bly. Reprinted by permission of Beacon Press, Boston.

Mysticism: A Study and an Anthology by F. C. Happold. Copyright © F. C. Happold, 1963, 1964, 1970. Reprinted by permission of Penguin Books, Ltd.

Mystics as a Force for Change by Sisirkumar Ghose. Copyright © 1981. Reprinted by permission of Theosophical Publishing House, Wheaton, Illinois.

"On a Clear Day (You Can See Forever)" (Burton Lane, Alan Jay Lerner). Copyright © 1965 Chappell & Co. All rights reserved. Used by permission.

Parenthesis in Eternity by Joel Goldsmith. Copyright © 1963 by Joel Goldsmith. Reprinted by permission of HarperCollins Publishers, Inc.

A Prison, a Paradise by Loran Hurnscot. Introduction by Kathleen Raine. Copyright © 1958 by Victor Gollancz, Ltd. Copyright renewed © 1986 by Kathleen Raine. Used by permission of Viking Penguin, a division of Penguin Books USA Inc.

The Relevance of Bliss by Nona Coxhead. Copyright © 1985. Reprinted by permission of John White, agent for the author.

The Root of the Matter by Margaret Isherwood. Copyright © English translation 1985 by Harper & Row, Publishers, Inc. Reprinted by permission of HarperCollins Publishers, Inc.

A Sleep of Prisoners by Christopher Fry. Copyright © 1951 by Christopher Fry; renewed 1979. Reprinted by permission of Oxford University Press, Inc.

Small Ecstacies, formerly *Awakening to the Good,* by Claire Myers Owens. Copyright © 1983 by Claire Myers Owens. Reprinted by permission of copyright holder, John White.

The Sound of Light by Irina Starr. Copyright © 1974 by Irina Starr. Reprinted by permission of Irina Starr, The Pilgrim's Path, P.O. Box 1632, Ojai, California 93024.

Talks With Great Composers by Arthur M. Abell. Copyright © 1955 by Philosophical Library. Reprinted by permission of Philosophical Library, Inc.

Through Mine Own Eyes by Katharine Trevelyan. Copyright © 1962 by Katharine Trevelyan. Reprinted by permission of Henry Holt and Company, Inc.

Watcher on the Hills by Raynor C. Johnson. Copyright © 1959. Reprinted by permission of Hodder & Stoughton Limited, London.

With the Door Open by Johannes Anker-Larsen, translated by Erwin and Pleasaunce von Gaisberg. Reprinted by permission of Macmillan Publishing Co.

You Can Find God by Starr Daily. Copyright © 1963. Reprinted by permission of Fleming H. Revell Company.

A Most Surprising Song

EXPLORING THE MYSTICAL EXPERIENCE

Awake, awake, the world is young
For all its weary years of thought
The starkest fights must still be fought,
The most surprising songs be sung!
                                    —James Elroy Flecker

Foreword

It gives me great pleasure to write this foreword to Louann Stahl's inspiring and informative book *A Most Surprising Song* in which she explores the mystical experience.

If you have had a mystical experience, if you would like to have one, or if you would just like to know what mysticism is, you will love this book. It tells what mysticism is, not by analyzing and defining it in abstract terms, though it does that too, but mainly by letting mystics themselves, famous mystics and unknown mystics, sing their surprising song. You cannot read this book without gaining a vividly realistic sense of the transforming, liberating power of the mystical experience. You see how it changes the mystics and you see how the mystics have changed the world.

If you have ever taken a college course in philosophy, you probably were taught that philosophy began with Pythagoras, who lived about 500 B.C. in Greece. Pythagoras was a mystic. He was also one of the first scientists and mathematicians we know anything about. If you took geometry in high school, one of the first things you learned was the Pythagorean theorem, "the square of the length of the hypotenuse of a right triangle equals the sum of the squares of the lengths of the other two sides."

Many of the greatest thinkers the human race has produced have had at least a touch of mysticism in their nature and in their systems of thought. Most mystics have been no weirder or stranger than writers or businessmen or housewives or kings or scientists.

The essence of mysticism is expressed in the mystical experience, the mystic vision. Mystics believe that they see themselves as they really are and see the world as it really is and see that they and the world are one. They see themselves and the world not as they seem to be to the rest of us, full of flaws and imperfections, but perfect and complete beyond all concepts of perfection and completeness. They declare that this is what we and our world are in our real nature.

Mysticism is more a way of life than a way of thought. The truth is a mystery, but not because it cannot be experienced. It can be experienced, but it cannot be described. Mystics burst through the veil of false appearances that enshroud us and catch a glimpse of themselves and the world as a shining glory. This glorious reality in which we are immersed is so glorious no one can describe it. You cannot conceive of it or analyze it or define it. You cannot put it into words or mathematical symbols, you can only say "It is."

You can see how close the relation of mysticism to Unity is when you realize that the central teaching of Unity is: There is only one Presence and one Power in the universe, God the good omnipotent. That is the central idea of religious mysticism.

Charles Fillmore was a mystic, and he said that Unity is a mysticism, but he said that it is a practical mysticism. Many years ago when I first heard him say that, I thought, How can there be a practical mysticism? The very essence of the mystical vision is that the material universe with its multiple appearances and cruelties and flaws is not the real world.

As Ms. Stahl points out, for the most part, the great mystics have been very practical human beings. Almost all the religions of the world have been founded by mystics. Some of these religions like Christianity, Buddhism, and Islam have been practical enough to guide hundreds of millions, even billions of human beings in ways that result in the good life.

Jesus was a mystic, Mohammed was a mystic, Buddha was a mystic, Lao-tzu was a mystic. So was Paul who, after his mystical vision on the road to Damascus, spread the

Christian religion around the world. Fifteen hundred years ago, St. Benedict fled from the voluptuous life of Rome and founded the first order of Christian monks. He set up such practical patterns and rules of life that they have been sufficient to govern monks and nuns ever since then and guide them into wonderfully productive lives. St. Francis, St. Teresa, St. Ignatius Loyola, all mystics, founded great orders that have been a principal source of growth of the Catholic church. John Knox and John Wesley, who founded great Protestant religions, were mystics.

Ms. Stahl persuades us that the mystic way is not an escape from life but an enrichment of life, a way of fulfillment. The mystic declares that the Real is One and so all the mystic's activities are directed to making that vision of oneness an actuality.

Significantly, Ms. Stahl shows us that the vision the mystic has of being one with the All that is One, may be a vision of the direction in which human evolution is meant to proceed, and is, indeed, actually proceeding. She points to the United Nations as a movement in that direction.

The United Nations, though it is more an attempt than an achievement, is nevertheless a vision of the world in a unified state. Whatever its failures may be, still it is bringing many different people together in a common effort to create a common world for all of us, a gentler, more benevolent, more abundant world. It may be only an immature beginning, but it is a beginning. The United Nations is a vision not unlike the mystic vision. It is the first step toward bringing into manifestation the world that the mystic tells us is the real world.

Finally, the mystic vision is of a world so splendid that all words fall short of describing it—a world peaceful, harmonious, orderly, productive, glorious, perfect, and complete, where we live the lives that God made us to live— radiantly alive, gloriously illumined; all of us unfettered, unbound, free, and all of us unified in spirit, all one with the one Transcendent Reality. In Unity, we express this same vision of what we and the world are meant to be by saying that we are to put on the Christ.

There is, in the Bible, an inspired description of the mystic vision. The writer writes: "I saw the holy city, new Jerusalem, coming down out of heaven from God, prepared as a bride adorned for her husband; and I heard a loud voice from the throne saying, 'Behold, the dwelling of God is with men. He will dwell with them, and they shall be his people, and God himself will be with them; he will wipe away every tear from their eyes, and death shall be no more, neither shall there be mourning nor crying nor pain any more, for the former things have passed away.'...

"Then came one of the seven angels ... saying, 'Come, I will show you the Bride, the wife of the Lamb.' And in the Spirit he carried me away to a great, high mountain, and showed me the holy city Jerusalem coming down out of heaven from God, having the glory of God, its radiance like a most rare jewel, like a jasper, clear as crystal....

"And the city has no need of sun or moon to shine upon it, for the glory of God is its light, and its lamp is the Lamb. By its light shall the nations walk; and the kings of the earth shall bring their glory into it, and its gates shall never be shut by day—and there shall be no night there" (Rev. 21:2-4, 9-11, 23-25).

This is the vision of the mystic, and is it not the hope of us all?

James Dillet Freeman
Lee's Summit, Missouri
September 1992

Preface

"There must be more to life. Surely this is not all there is." Some stirrings in the soul send up this message from time to time. We all recognize it. Life has often disappointed us. There are times when those sun-filled childhood expectations seem to have dried up in our hearts. And yet, before we have sent down taproots to the inward springs that might nourish us, we have made an all too early and accommodating peace with what we call "the reality of life." Wordsworth said it well. "The World is too much with us; late and soon, / Getting and spending, we lay waste our powers; / ...We have given our hearts away." The words as well as the lives of the great mystics would attest to the truth of Wordsworth's poem. For there are those who have found more.

There are those who have found profound peace and a glory incomprehensible to most of us. They speak of a love which we can only contemplate with awe.

There are those who have found meaning in life—the want of which gnaws at our souls, if we have accepted the mundane "realities of living" as "all there is."

There are those who have found a way. But the journey is an inward and not an outward one. The first steps, they agree, are often easy—a light flashed upon the path. As the road progresses, it can become difficult and dark. But that intoxicating light seen ahead calls the pilgrim forward— forward to a new life, a new freedom (and yet not new, having been with us always). An Indian mystic of the ninth century, Bayezid Bistami, remarked, "For thirty years I went in search of God, and when at the end of that time I opened my eyes, I discovered that it was he who had been looking for me."

Beyond the love, peace, and joy that pervade the song of the mystics (I say song because the truth they have found is so luminous and lyrical that "message" does not properly convey their meaning) their experiences point to a deeper level of reality. The nature of reality revealed in that indescribable light discloses paradox—but a paradox full of hope. We are many they say, but we are also One. Underneath the manifold manifestation of life there exists an essential unity of all creation and a unity of all creation with the Divine.

Skeptics say there can be no proof that the treasure we seek in following the mystic path is really there, that it is not a delusion. The skeptics are right in one sense: there can be no strictly scientific proof, for the knowledge of which the mystics speak is a personal revelation. They say they can only point the direction; they can only draw the map of the inward journey that will lead us to the "pearl of great price."

In fact, the very characteristic of pointing the way rather than proclaiming truths for others to believe is a sign of the true mystic. "Go where I have been if you would find true life," says the mystic, "for the reality that I have found is too awesome, too mighty. It cannot be expressed, it can only be experienced." Yet point the way he must, for, as the great Jewish theologian Martin Buber said, the mystic is compelled to speak because "the Word burns in him."

Also, the conviction with which the mystics hold the knowledge of their experience is unbendable. For the most part they are men and women whose lives have confirmed their intelligence, their maturity, their moral fiber, and their dedication to truth. Indeed, they have been some of the greatest personages throughout history, including the founders of most of the major religions.

However, even lacking "proof," our journey would not be a fool's errand. There are many indications of the validity of the mystical experience and the nature of reality it reveals. As ancient as the oldest religion, the mystical experience transcends time, culture, religion, geography, gender, and age. The words of the mystics span the globe and speak to us from every time, from every religion, from every culture, from men and women, adults and children. The message is often so similar that we are shocked to realize that there could have been no contact between most of these people.

This book is an exploration into the mystical experience: its characteristics; how it is perceived emotionally, physically, and mentally; the nature of reality revealed in the mystical illumination; the catalysts that trigger the experience; and its significance for both the individual and society. I have used, where possible, the words of the mystics themselves, not only to describe their experiences but also to share their attempts to express what, ultimately, the mystic vision has meant to them. It is my hope that in some small way their testimony will bring hope where there is despair, light where there is darkness. Their hearts on fire with the glory of a transcending love and joy, they have left a light shining for us.

The Imprisoned Splendor

Five Cases of
Mystical Illumination

*Truth is within ourselves; it takes no rise
From outward things, whate'er you may believe.
There is an inmost centre in us all,
Where truth abides in fulness; and around,
Wall upon wall, the gross flesh hems it in,
This perfect, clear perception—which is truth.
A baffling and perverting carnal mesh
Binds it, and makes all error; and to KNOW
Rather consists in opening out a way
Whence the imprisoned splendour may escape,
Than in effecting entry for a light
Supposed to be without.*

—Robert Browning

Although often confused with other phenomena, the mystical experience is a direct contact with a Transcendent Reality which most mystics call God. However, since the word *God* has so many different connotations, others prefer terms such as the Ultimate Reality, the Undifferentiated Unity, the Source of our Being, and so on. But, whatever the name, this Transcendent Reality is perceived to be the most joyful, most loving, and most real experience ever known by those fortunate enough to have met with it. The experience brings with it a sense of peace as well as an exultation, and a feeling of certainty and well-being that might best be expressed in the words of Julian of Norwich who, in the fifteenth century during her encounter with this Transcendent Reality, was assured, "All will be well, and all will be well, and every kind of thing will be well."[1]

The following stories are about the mystical experiences of five people, ranging from a convicted criminal to a religious saint. They illustrate both the profound nature and commonality of what they encounter and reassure us that it is an experience open to all.

The indescribable light lit up the dark prison cell where Starr Daily, a hardened criminal, lay on the stone floor in solitary confinement. The light, seemingly coming from nowhere, illumined the darkness completely. With the light came a presence. Starr Daily described his experience in these words:

> He [Christ] came toward me, his lips moving, but not vocally. He paused near my side ... and looked down, deep down into my eyes [they were sunk in black sockets], as though through them he were trying to penetrate my soul. In all my life I had never

seen or felt such love in the human eye as now glowed and radiated in his eyes. Nor had I ever felt myself so utterly helpless in the captivity of love. By some mysterious faculty of perception, which operated in the midst of my dream, I seemed to know clearly that I was submerged in Reality; that I was seeing and feeling something that would influence my life throughout all eternity.[2]

Another day, out of solitary confinement and at work in the prison garment shop, Starr Daily prayed for help to ward off his old habits of resentment and self-pity. At this moment he "touched upon another world," a world that he tried to describe.

It was the same garment shop, and yet it was not the same. The voices and machines blended into the most exquisite harmonies and musical cadences. At no point could I discern a jarring note in this symphony of sounds. The dust and lint in the air became myriad units of unearthly radiance, as though each of the millions of tiny particles stood out separately and moved in perfect waves of rhythm.

I looked around at my fellow workers. Their faces were aglow. The shopkeeper, a grim, taciturn man, seemed to walk about in an aura of glorious light.

The experience arrived suddenly and departed in like manner, but my destructive thought-world was transformed. All fatigue went out of me. I worked easily, with little or no lost motion.[3]

Young girls in white dresses, sitting in the front pew of a South African church waiting for their confirmation ceremony to begin, were giggling and distracted by the presence of the young boys, uncomfortably dressed up with hair slicked down, fidgeting in the opposite pew. The boys and the girls were waiting for their turn, as rehearsed, to go up one by one and kneel at the altar where the Bishop of Natal, who had come to town especially for this occasion, would perform the ceremony.

One young girl, Moyra Caldecott, going through the preliminary service by rote with thoughts "all over the place—certainly not on anything profoundly religious," was caught in a very unexpected experience.

> It was my turn. He put his hand on my head ... I didn't hear what he said but ...
> I suddenly seemed to cease to be me (that is, in the sense of "me" I had thought I was—living in a particular house, in a particular street, going to a particular school). I felt the most incredible flow of energy and power coursing through me and had, what I believe to be, an experience of Timeless Reality ... of consciousness that took in everything without limit ... but reacted to nothing except in the sense of "knowing ... and loving".
> The Bishop must have had his hand on my head for no more than a few seconds—but one could live a whole lifetime and not gain as much insight as I gained in this one beautiful, devastating moment.
> I stood up and went back to my place in the pew as I had been trained to do ... trembling, shaken.[4]

Three soldiers, revolvers in hand, rushed into the peaceful Villa Santa Lucia in Malaga. They wanted Sir Peter Chalmers Mitchell, a retired British scientist, and Arthur Koestler, then a young journalist covering the Spanish Civil War. Mitchell and Koestler were waiting, knowing that Franco's troops would overrun the city at any moment. The soldiers bound Koestler's wrists and forced the two men into a car at gunpoint. They were driven through streets where other prisoners were being summarily executed against stone walls. Koestler was taken to a Spanish prison where for three months he never knew if he would survive the night. Between the hours of midnight and 2 a.m., prisoners from all the cells around him were marched off to execution, as many as seventeen in one night.

Living in this shadow of death, Koestler noticed a change in consciousness, especially during the three occasions when he was sure death was at hand. "I had benefited from the well known phenomenon of a split consciousness," said Koestler, "a dream-like, dazed self-estrangement which separated the conscious self from the acting self—the former becoming a detached observer, the latter an automaton."[5]

Koestler spent much time at the recessed window in cell 40 in the Seville prison. While standing there, he had many revelations. Among them was the following, which happened after he had scratched on the prison wall Euclid's proof that the number of primes is infinite, a proof which he said always filled him with a deep aesthetic satisfaction.

> ... (these) scribbled symbols ... represented one of the rare cases where a meaningful and comprehensive statement about the infinite is arrived at by precise and finite means. ... The significance of this swept over me like a wave.

... I must have stood there for some minutes, entranced, with a wordless awareness that "this is perfect—perfect"; until I noticed some slight mental discomfort nagging at the back of my mind—some trivial circumstance that marred the perfection of the moment.... Then I remembered the nature of that irrelevant annoyance: I was, of course, in prison and might be shot. But this was immediately answered by a feeling whose verbal translation would be: "So what? is that all? have you got nothing more serious to worry about?"—an answer so spontaneous, fresh and amused as if the intruding annoyance had been the loss of a collar-stud. Then I was floating on my back in a river of peace, under bridges of silence. It came from nowhere and flowed nowhere. Then there was no river and no I. The I had ceased to exist.

...When I say "the I had ceased to exist," I refer to a concrete experience that is verbally as incommunicable as the feeling aroused by a piano concerto, yet just as real—only much more real. In fact, its primary mark is the sensation that this state is more real than any other one has experienced before—that for the first time the veil has fallen and one is in touch with "real reality," the hidden order of things ... normally obscured by layers of irrelevancy."[6]

For a year the elderly nun had been ill, suffering greatly, and now she was close to death. Another Sister, with whom she shared great affection, had come to her bedside to nurse and comfort her. However, she had long been aware that her dear friend was comforted elsewhere and seemed to have an extraordinary inner strength. Moved to know the secret of the dying nun's peace and joy, her companion begged that she share the source of her comfort and consolation.

With that question, a flood of memories of a night many years ago entered the dying nun's mind. She asked to be left alone for a little while. After the singing of the compline, her friend returned to her bedside, whereupon the elderly nun said, "Lift me up and give me some water in my mouth so that I can speak; then I will tell you what you will be glad to hear." This is the story that she told:

Sofia, a young nun in the second year of her vows, at the feast of the holy nativity, had stayed in the choir after midnight mass. Leaning against a prayer stand behind the altar, she poured out her soul to God. "While I was praying," the now elderly nun told her companion, "my former life came into my mind, how much time and how long I had spent in the world in frivolous pursuits. And I began especially to contemplate and consider the faithlessness I had thereby shown to God, that I had cared so negligently for the noble and dignified treasure of my noble soul." The pain she felt at this was like a wound in her heart, and she was overcome with remorse. She confided to her friend "all bodily strength ... failed ... and I ... fell into a swoon, so that I could neither see nor hear nor speak."

When young Sofia awoke, and not wanting to be found like this, she struggled to her bed in the dormitory, made the sign of the Cross and said the verse *In manus tuas*. After repeating this prayer she immediately had the following revelation:

> I saw that a light, beautiful and blissful
> beyond measure, was coming from heaven, and
> it surrounded me and shone through me and
> illuminated me entirely, and my heart was
> transformed all of a sudden and filled with an

unspeakable and strange joy, so that I utterly and completely forgot all the misery and torment that I had ever known until this time. And in the light and in the joy, I saw and sensed that my God was taken up from my heart ... and there it was given me to see my soul clearly and particularly with spiritual vision, as I have never seen anything with physical eyes, and all its form and grace and beauty was shown to me fully. And what marvels I saw and recognized in it, all humans together could not put into words.

Her companion was so moved at the older nun's words that she begged her to go on in her description of the soul. Gathering strength, Sofia answered with these words:

If all the stars in the sky were as big and beautiful as the sun, and if they were all shining together, all their splendor could not compare with the beauty my soul had. And it seemed to me that a splendor went out from me that illuminated the whole world, and a blissful day dawned over the whole earth. And in this light which was my soul, I saw God blissfully shining, as a beautiful light shines out of a beautiful radiant lamp, and I saw that he nestled up to my soul so lovingly and so kindly that he was wholly united with it and it with him.

This blessing lasted for eight days and was the beginning of the many graces that Sofia von Klingnau of the Toss Convent in Germany in the thirteenth century received from God.[7]

The shoemaker of Görlitz had had an unremarkable but pleasant life. As a young boy, he had been a shepherd on Londs Krone Hill, but since his dreamy and thoughtful nature did not incline him toward agriculture, Jacob Boehme was apprenticed to a shoemaker. Eventually he became master of his own shop, married, and had four sons.

Although prudent and prosperous in his work, he was religiously inclined and much given to deep thought and speculation on the nature of things. His sparkling, gray-blue eyes would often seem to withdraw to search an inner world. One day in the year 1600, while working in the shop, these penetrating eyes fell by chance on a burnished pewter dish "which reflected the sunshine with such marvellous splendor that he fell into an inward ecstasy."[8]

Accompanying the magnificent light that filled the room, there came to Boehme an inward illumination "and it seemed to him as if he could now look into the principles and deepest foundation of things."[9] Thinking that his experience was only fancy and imagination, he walked outside to clear his mind. Quite the opposite happened. The vision persisted and became even clearer. A veil seemed lifted from nature, and he saw that the grass and flowers were animated by living forces that flowed through everything. "Going abroad in the fields to a green before Neys Gate, at Görlitz, he there sat down and, viewing the herbs and grass of the field in his inward light, he saw into their essences, use and properties."[10] The mysteries of life unfolded before him. Although this experience gave Jacob much joy, he thanked God, returned home and said nothing of his wonderful illumination.

For ten years Jacob persevered in his trade, prospered in his business, and led a good and productive life. However, his thoughts were ever on the deeper mysteries of life, and he longed for greater understanding and vision than that which had been granted to him. His moments of vision came, but did not stay. When speaking of this experience, he later said, "The first fire was but a beginning and not a ... lasting light." He still could not reconcile the world he saw—the inequity, suffering, evil, and hypocrisy—with the world revealed in his vision. His intense desire for enlightenment—to know God—was so great that one day he stormed "the gates of hell."

> In this affliction ... I elevated my spirit ... up into God, as with a great storm or onset, wrapping up my whole heart and mind, as also all my thoughts and whole will....
> When in my resolved zeal I gave so hard an assault ... upon God ... suddenly my spirit did break through ... into the innermost moving of the Deity, and there I was embraced in love as a bridegroom embraces his dearly beloved bride."[11]

Boehme described in his first book, *Aurora*, the import and nature of this experience, stating that the gate was opened to him so that "in one quarter of an hour I saw and knew more than if I had been many years together at an university. For I saw and knew the being of all things, the Byss and the Abyss, and the eternal generation of the holy Trinity."[12] According to his biographer, Hartmann, "that which in former visions had appeared to him chaotic and multifarious was now recognized by him as a unity, like a harp of many strings, of which each string is a separate instrument, while the whole is only one harp." Now he knew more clearly the divine order of nature, and "how from the trunk of the tree of life spring different branches."[13] After this Boehme became impressed with the necessity of writing down what had become revealed to him.

His revelations continued and write he did, in spite of the persecution by his local church and his own mental and physical hardships. Eventually his words were translated into many languages and widely influenced the development of religious thought. His life and words exemplify the highest religious aspirations of seventeenth century Europe, especially England, and today he is still studied by serious students of metaphysics everywhere as one of the greatest Protestant mystics, the German cobbler, "a God taught seer."

Most people who have a mystical experience do not become religious saints as did Jacob Boehme, but their lives are nevertheless deeply and forever affected.

Starr Daily, his life transformed by his prison experience, became an internationally known author of inspirational literature. Moyra Caldecott married, had children, and led an ordinary life, but one punctuated and deepened by mystical insight. The experiences of Arthur Koestler in cell 40 profoundly shaped his thought as a philosopher-scientist and author, and his writing made a significant impact on the thought of his time. Until the recent publishing of the German Sister-books of the Toss Convent of the thirteenth century, the revelation of Sofia von Klingnau remained in obscurity. Her life of dedication to God was reborn and uplifted in joy, beauty, and love.

A Sense Sublime

Sublime

Patterns of
Mystical Experience

I have felt
A presence that disturbs me with the joy
Of elevated thoughts; a sense sublime
Of something far more deeply interfused,
Whose dwelling is the light of setting suns,
And the round ocean and the living air,
And the blue sky, and in the mind of man:
A motion and a spirit, that impels
All thinking things, all objects of all thought,
and rolls through all things.

—William Wordsworth

Enlightenment, mystical experience, cosmic consciousness—are these words too strange, concepts too foreign for the more earthbound mind to contemplate? Not really. Many of us have no doubt felt, with William Wordsworth, "a presence that disturbs me with the joy / Of elevated thoughts." This feeling exists even if we cannot or do not aspire to "the mystic act of union" that Evelyn Underhill calls the "crown of man's conscious ascent towards the Absolute."[1] This contact with a Transcendent Reality, variously called the Ultimate Source, the Ground of our Being, and God, *is* a mystical experience, a step toward cosmic consciousness. In some degree, it is an enlightenment, as small as an intuition, as large as a complete revelation of life's mysteries.

Documented by countless individuals throughout time, from every culture, religion, and race, the mystical experience has a recurring pattern that is easily recognized. While often interpreted according to religious and cultural predisposition, the core experiences are often indistinguishable from each other. This recurring pattern has been a prime reason why many people have taken these experiences seriously and attributed such validity to them. The occurrence of the mystical experience at all times and places and the similarities between the statements of so many mystics all the world over are significant facts to many who study this phenomenon. This suggests that there is an aspect of reality with which these people come in contact in their mystical experience which they have difficulty describing in the language of everyday life. "Earthly language," said Jacob Boehme, "is entirely insufficient to describe what there is of joy, happiness, and loveliness contained in the inner wonders of God."[2] However, most mystics feel compelled to share their discoveries in writing, and since these stories are so fascinating, there is no lack of researchers to study them.

At this point, we may ask: Who is, and who is not, a

mystic? The broadest definition, given by Evelyn Underhill, suggests that anyone who has experienced a transcendent union with the Ultimate Reality or anyone who believes in the possibility of such union and aspires to it is a mystic. However, in this discussion, we shall deal only with those who have had a mystical experience.

Maurice Bucke was a Canadian physician of the nineteenth century. He believed that mystics had attained an advanced form of consciousness which, through evolution, will become more common until eventually it will be attained by all people. This new, advanced stage of consciousness, or "Cosmic Consciousness," will bring with it an intellectual enlightenment which alone would place humanity on a new plane of existence. Characterized by the realization of "the oneness of the Universe," a sense of "the presence in it and throughout it of the Creator," this advanced consciousness would free humankind of "all fears of evil, of disaster or death," and would allow it "to comprehend that Love is the rule and basis of the Cosmos."[3] Bucke began his historical study of mystics after his own profound mystical experience:

> It was in the early spring, at the beginning of his thirty-sixth year. He [Bucke] and two friends had spent the evening reading Wordsworth, Shelley, Keats, Browning, and especially Whitman. They parted at midnight, and he had a long drive in a hansom.... His mind, deeply under the influence of the ideas, images and emotions called up by the reading and talk of the evening, was calm and peaceful. He was in a state of quiet, almost passive enjoyment. All at once, without warning of any kind, he found himself wrapped around as it were by a flame-colored cloud. For an instant he thought of fire, some sudden conflagration

in the great city; the next, he knew that the light was within himself. Directly afterwards came upon him a sense of exultation, of immense joyousness accompanied or immediately followed by an intellectual illumination quite impossible to describe. Into his brain streamed one momentary lightning-flash of the Brahmic Splendor which has ever since lightened his life; upon his heart fell one drop of Brahmic Bliss, leaving thenceforward for always an aftertaste of heaven. Among other things he did not come to believe, *he saw and knew* [italics the author's] that the Cosmos is not dead matter but a living Presence, that the soul of man is immortal, that the universe is so built and ordered that without any peradventure all things work together for the good of each and all, that the foundation principle of the world is what we call love and that the happiness of every one is in the long run absolutely certain. He claims that he learned more within the few seconds during which the illumination lasted than in previous months or even years of study, and that he learned much that no study could ever have taught.[4]

Maurice Bucke was not alone in being led toward a study of mysticism by his own startling and unexplainable experience, nor was he alone in the conclusions he drew. F. C. Happold, a British schoolmaster who served in World War I, had a series of experiences which led him into a study of mysticism, and he, too, concluded that the elevated consciousness of the mystic was a step in man's evolution. In the following, he speculates on the course of evolution:

May it not be the growth of an ever higher form of consciousness, spreading out ever wider and wider, until it embraces more and more of mankind ... which will result in an ability to see aspects of the universe as yet only faintly glimpsed? And, if that be so, may we not see in the mystics the forerunners of a type of consciousness, which will become more and more common as mankind ascends higher and higher up the ladder of evolution? [5]

At the time of his first experience, Happold knew nothing of mystics or of mystical experience. In the following narration, he describes, however, many of the same elements that appear in Bucke's narration:

It happened in my room in Peterhouse on the evening of 1 February 1913, when I was an undergraduate at Cambridge. If I say that Christ came to me I should be using conventional words which would carry no precise meaning; for Christ comes to men and women in different ways.... There was, however, no sensible vision. There was just the room, with its shabby furniture and the fire burning in the grate and the red-shaded lamp on the table. But the room was filled by a Presence, which in a strange way was both about me and within me, like light or warmth. I was overwhelmingly possessed by Someone who was not myself, and yet I felt I was more myself than I had ever been before. I was filled with an intense happiness, and almost unbearable joy, such as I had never known before and have never known since. And over all was a deep sense of peace and security and certainty.[6]

More experiences followed, but the one that occurred in 1916, during the Battle of the Somme, is particularly poignant.

> I crouched in the darkness in a front-line trench, which was nothing but a muddy ditch, stinking with unburied corpses, amid a tangle of shell-holes. At dawn my battalion was due to attack. I watched the slow movement of the luminous dial of my wrist-watch, dreading the moment when I must get up and lead my men forward towards the German lines. And suddenly, with absolute certainty, I knew that I was utterly safe.... [It was not] the sort of fatalism not uncommon among fighting men in action. Rather it was a vivid sense of being completely safe physically. When the thunder of the barrage broke I went forward quite unafraid.[7]

Happold saw in that event a similarity to a later experience when he was concerned with the health of his wife

> [It] happened to me on the evening of 18 April 1936, the evening of the day before my son was born. My first child had been still-born and, as I lay in bed, I was very anxious about my wife and much disturbed in mind. And then a great peace came over me. I was conscious of a lovely, unexplainable pattern in the whole texture of things, a pattern of which everyone and everything was a part; and weaving the pattern was a Power; and that Power was what we faintly call Love. I realized that we are not lonely atoms in a cold, unfriendly, indifferent

universe, but that each of us is linked up in a rhythm, of which we may be unconscious, and which we can never really know, but to which we can submit ourselves trustfully and unreservedly.[8]

Perhaps Pierre Teilhard de Chardin, a Jesuit priest, religious mystic, and renowned paleontologist, spoke most eloquently to modern mankind of the evolution of human consciousness. He saw scientific research as a part of the process which strives to discover the universal in the particular, and religion and science as two phases of one complete act of knowledge. The human person, able to merge reason and religion, is, he believed, the "leading shoot of evolution,"[9] destined for "not only survival but also *super-life.*"[10] His life as well as his research did much to prove that the mystic vision and scientific research were reconcilable.

In the following passage, written toward the end of his life, Father Teilhard reveals the mystical spirit that has grown within him:

> *Throughout* my life, *by means of* my life, the world has little by little caught fire in my sight until, aflame all around me, it has become almost completely luminous from within.... Such has been my experience in contact with the earth—the diaphany of the Divine at the heart of the universe on fire ... Christ; his heart; a fire: capable of penetrating everywhere and, gradually, spreading everywhere.[11]

Even though mystical experiences vary, we are able to recognize a pattern. First, the experience is lived, participated in, not comprehended with the mind alone, while the sense of *reality* and the sense of being at last *awake* is so great that normal consciousness seems a pale imitation. Second, it is an experience of overwhelming joy and love, often accompanied by a preternatural light, brilliant and luminous beyond measure. Third, the mystic experiences the "peace of God, which passes all understanding" (Phil. 4:7), along with a sense of the unity of all creation—a unity underlying a wondrous and awesome diversity. Fourth, while an illumination of the meaning of life is often a part of the mystic's experience, the explanations they attempt are most often obscured in paradoxes the human mind cannot untangle. Inevitably, the mystics tell us that the experience is ineffable, our concepts and language simply cannot embrace it. Their tongues are tied, as that of the man who ascended from Plato's Cave. Fifth, time as we know it is transcended; the mystical experience exists outside of time in an "eternal now."

It is compelling to know that the way to a consciousness of God has been paved for us by those who have been called "our lovely forerunners." Most of us are not quite ready to take giant steps into *reality.* The "door" remains open, however, and we can proceed gently on our way, or "storm the gates of hell" with Jacob Boehme.

However we proceed, the mystics assure us that we shall find the way and that we shall be awakened to a new and embryonic consciousness of a divine reality. As Evelyn Underhill has written, "The germ of that same transcendent life, the spring of the amazing energy which enables the great mystic to rise to freedom and dominate his world, is latent in all of us; an integral part of our humanity."[12]

CHAPTER THREE

Awake in Heaven

Mysticism Evoked by Nature's Glories

*Y*our enjoyment of the world is never right, till every morning you awake in Heaven; see yourself in your Father's Palace; and look upon the skies, the earth, and the air as Celestial Joys: having such a reverend esteem of all, as if you were among the Angels.

—*Thomas Traherne*

Among the most beautiful passages in the Bible are the first two lines from Psalm 19, "The heavens declare the glory of God; and the firmament sheweth his handywork" (Ps. 19 KJV). Of all the mystics, perhaps the most joyful are those who see and experience the glory of God in all God's creation. Those we affectionately call the nature mystics have shared with us their joy and ecstasy in poetry, prose, and other works of art. The Romantics come first to mind, such as Blake, Wordsworth, Keats, Shelley, and Coleridge; but writers and artists who are able to see more deeply and clearly the Divine in the universe abound in all cultures and ages. The ecstatic joy that surges through them is intoxicating. When John Masefield says in his poem, "I thought all earthly creatures knelt / From rapture of the joy I felt," we, too, feel this joyous surge in us. Although not always going to the depths of the religious mystics, the nature mystics may have brought to us more of what they experienced.

But the mysticism that is evoked by the glories of creation is not the sole purview of writers and artists. It is simply the most common type of mysticism. Countless numbers of people have had mystical experiences triggered by the beauties and wonders of nature. Furthermore, the experiences of the nature mystic often more completely encompass those aspects usually associated with mystical experience—the joy, beauty, unity, peace, and even the sense of knowing and timelessness.

The experience of an English woman, as reported by Nona Coxhead in *The Relevance of Bliss*, illustrates how complete a mystical experience triggered by nature can be. Wendy Rose-Neill, a medical journalist, psychotherapist, and avid gardener, was not a religious person in the accepted sense. In fact, she considered herself a radical humanist. One autumn day while tending her garden, she felt unusually relaxed and contemplative and became very aware of the beauty around her: the birds, the breeze coming softly through the leaves and touching her face, the scent of grass and flowers. She followed a sudden impulse to lie facedown on the grass, and felt energy flow through her from the earth. This is the rest of her experience:

> The boundary between my physical self and my surroundings seemed to dissolve and my feeling of separation vanished. In a strange way I felt blended into a total unity with the earth, as if I were made of it and it of me. I was aware of the blades of grass between my fingers and touching my face, and I was overwhelmed by a force which seemed to penetrate every fibre of my being.
>
> I felt as if I had suddenly come alive for the first time—as if I were awakening from a long deep sleep into a real world. I remember feeling that a veil had been lifted from my eyes and everything came into focus, although my head was still on the grass. Whatever else I believed, I realized that I was surrounded by an incredible loving energy, and that everything, both living and non-living, is bound inextricably with a kind of consciousness which I cannot describe in words.
>
> Although the experience could not have lasted for more than a few minutes, it seemed endless—as if I were in some kind of suspended eternal state of understanding. Then it passed and I remained still and quiet on the lawn, trying to absorb what had happened and not quite believing that it was real. A profound feeling of joy and peace is what I recall afterwards from those extraordinary moments.[1]

This was not the only mystical experience that Wendy

Rose-Neill was to have, nor was it an incident apart a without meaning for her life. "Their general effect," she said, "has been to enrich the quality of my life and to give me a sense of continuity and meaning which has taken me through times of great personal crisis, when it seemed that everything was crumbling away." She also claimed to have gained a profound sense of wonder and mystery about the earth and the universe and an "ever-deepening respect for all of life."[2]

Not surprisingly, the child is often a natural nature mystic. Many people have glimmerings of strange and wonderful experiences of nature from their childhood which have slowly faded in the memory. Wordsworth expresses well the conditioning effect of "the real world" upon the youthful nature.

> Our birth is but a sleep and a forgetting:
> The Soul that rises with us, our life's Star,
> Hath had elsewhere its setting,
> And cometh from afar:
> Not in entire forgetfulness,
> And not in utter nakedness,
> But trailing clouds of glory do we come
> From God, who is our home:
> Heaven lies about us in our infancy!
> Shades of the prison-house begin to close
> Upon the growing Boy;
> But He beholds the light, and whence it flows,
> He sees it in his joy;
> The Youth who daily farther from the east
> Must travel, still is Nature's Priest,
> And by the vision splendid
> Is on his way attended;
> At length the Man perceives it die away,
> And fade into the light of common day.

And yet some people remember vividly the magic of their childhood years, and there are even those who have lost the "vision splendid" from their youth and have found it once again.

The poet John Masefield was able to return in memory to his early childhood when the whole world was filled with ecstatic beauty. "Known by me," he wrote in his auto-biography, "to be ... only the shadow of something much more beautiful, very, very near, and almost to be reached, where there was nothing but beauty itself in ecstasy, undying, inexhaustible."[3] Although barely five years old at the time, Masefield remembered the following moments:

> I entered that greater life; and that life entered into me with a delight that I can never forget....
> Something, I know not what, in the very reality of the joy, told me that this could not be talked about, it was too intense for that:... But from that wonderful hour, I had a life for myself, better than any life of men; and for some years I lived in that life, and could enter it at will, or almost at will, unknown to anybody.[4]

However, the "prison house," in the form of great sorrows, began to close around him, and Masefield lost the ability to experience this reality. For some time he despaired and even thought he had been "damned," as elders suggested would be his fate. With time, however, he found again the "radiant splendour" of that life he had earlier experienced within himself and in the world. In his autobiography, *So Long to Learn*, he expressed his faith in its reality. "I believe that life to be the source of all that is of glory or goodness in this world; and that modern man, not knowing that life, is dwelling in death."[5]

Myrtle Fillmore, co-founder with her husband Charles of Unity School of Christianity, would as a child retreat to a favorite shaded nook along the banks of Big Walnut Creek near her home in Ohio. In her special place, she sat beneath the willows and oaks and watched the small animals and birds, while listening to their chatter and songs.

> Mary Caroline [Myrtle] would tuck her hands under her head, with her face turned skyward, and soon she *wasn't there at all.* No, she would be way up among the fleecy, changeful, melting clouds. She would be among the swaying branches of the green trees, among the birds that sang and soared—among whatever there was up there to be among. Somehow, she would seem to be *one* with all that was. Then suddenly her soul and body would be reunited and she would be aware that the process had taken place.[6]

During her adult life, Myrtle Fillmore was to continue to have these blissful, mystical moments inspired by the beauties of nature when she felt part of all she saw—and part of God.

Henry David Thoreau, mystic, naturalist, and philosopher, had similar ecstatic experiences in his childhood. Although he remained a mystic throughout his life, in his *Journal*, he described the experiences of his youth with special feeling.

> My life was ecstasy. In youth, before I lost any of my senses, I can remember that I was all alive, and inhabited my body with inexpress- ible satisfaction; ... This earth was the most glorious musical instrument, and I was audience to its strains. To have such sweet

impressions made on us, such ecstasies begotten of the breezes! I can remember how I was astonished. I said to myself—I said to others,—"There comes into my mind such an indescribable, infinite, all-absorbing, divine, heavenly pleasure, a sense of elevation and expansion, and [I] have had nought to do with it. I perceive that I am dealt with by superior powers."[7]

Thoreau's "heavenly pleasure" echoes through the accounts of numerous mystics who seize the most profound term they know to describe the majesty of their experience. Over and over in descriptions of the mystical experience, we encounter such expressions as: "It was like heaven," or "I was in heaven."

The following is a report of an older woman telling of her experience as a girl of nine, which was triggered by the beauty of nature. On a clear and shining day she had taken her baby sister into a favorite meadow.

I took off my shoes and stockings, carried the baby across the stream, and laid her down gently under the lime trees, which were in bloom and smelling most beautifully. There were soft white clouds in the sky, but the sun was shining. Everything was very quiet save for the munching of the lazy, melancholy cows, and the gentle burble of the brook, whose banks were covered with lacy meadow-sweet, pink willow-herb, and sky-blue forget-me-nots. Suddenly the Thing happened, and, as everybody knows, it cannot be described in words. The Bible phrase "I saw the heavens open" seems as good as any if it is not taken literally. I remember saying to myself, in awe and rapture, "So it's like this: now I know what Heaven is like, now I know what they mean in church." The words of the 23rd Psalm came into my head and I began repeating them: "He maketh me lie down in green pastures; he leadeth me beside the still waters." Soon It faded and I was alone in the meadow with the baby and the brook and the sweet-smelling lime trees. But although it had passed and only the earthly beauty remained, I was filled with a great gladness; I had seen the "far distances".[8]

This rapture brought on by nature is not, of course, reserved for the very young; they just seem to be more open to the pararational occurrences of life. Nevertheless, the experience of being "in heaven" is also spoken of in many adult accounts of mystical experiences. The following is an account of a mature man in the prime of a successful career, who is still questioning and seeking a fuller and more authentic life. This passage is from his autobiography, *My Quest for God.*

One brilliant Sunday morning, my wife and boys went to the Unitarian Chapel in Maccles-field. I felt it impossible to accompany them— as though to leave the sunshine on the hills, and go down there to the chapel, would be for the time an act of spiritual suicide. And I felt such need for new inspiration and expansion in my life. So, very reluctantly and sadly, I left my wife and boys to go down into the town, while I went further up into the hills with my stick and my dog. In the loveliness of the morning, and the beauty of the hills and valleys, I soon lost my sense of sadness and regret. For nearly an hour I walked along the road to the "Cat and

Fiddle," and then returned. On the way back, suddenly, without warning, I felt that I was in Heaven—an inward state of peace and joy and assurance indescribably intense, accompanied with a sense of being bathed in a warm glow of light, as though the external condition had brought about the internal effect—a feeling of having passed beyond the body, though the scene around me stood out more clearly and as if nearer to me than before, by reason of the illumination in the midst of which I seemed to be placed. This deep emotion lasted, though with decreasing strength, until I reached home, and for some time after, only gradually passing away.[9]

J. Trevor, who wrote the above passage, speaks of being bathed in a warm glow of light. That light—supernal, preternatural, warm, glowing, or brilliant—figures in almost all mystical experiences. Blessed John Ruysbroeck from the thirteenth century, one of the great religious mystics, said of souls touched by the divine that "their bare understanding is drenched through by the Eternal Brightness, even as the air is drenched through by the sunshine."[10] This light seems not to be only in the atmosphere, but also to radiate from everything surrounding the person having the experience.

Contemporary writer Irina Starr had been on an inner spiritual journey for some time when she had some remarkable and extended experiences which began with this amazing light:

The radiance which permeated my eyelids and suffused the entire room caught me unawares. Everything around me had come to life in some wondrous way and was lit from within with a moving, living, radiance....

I was obviously seeing with vision other than the purely physical, but what I saw did not conflict with what my ordinary vision registered .... I saw objects in the ordinary way as well as with some extraordinary extension of the visual faculty; I saw into them with an inner vision and it was this inner sight which revealed the commonplace objects around me to be of the most breathtaking beauty....

The one thing which was, above all, significant was that everything was literally *alive*; the light was living, pulsating, and in some way I could not quite grasp, *intelligent*. The true substance of all I could see was this living light, beautiful beyond words. This awareness of beauty so intense as to be nearly unbearable was not to leave me for the four days in which I beheld the world with extended sight.[11]

This extended vision is unusual but not without precedent, especially among the religious mystics who have sought continual oneness with God through the "mystic path." Jacob Boehme, we are told, was "surrounded by a divine Light for seven days, and stood in the highest contemplation and Kingdom of Joy."

The outward light seen by the mystics is often associated by them with the inward illumination that they receive. Claire Myers Owens, a self-described "privileged American housewife," had an intense illumination after the appearance of a "a great golden light." She had been suffering a despondency and despair due to an acute empathy for the enormous suffering in the world and the potential for unprecedented destruction that exists. In her book *Awakening to the Good* (later republished under the title *Small Ecstasies*), she describes the revelation that came one quiet morning as she was working at her writing desk:

> Suddenly the entire room was filled with a great golden light, the whole world was filled with nothing but light. There was nothing anywhere except this effulgent light and my own small kernel of the self. The ordinary "I" ceased to exist. Nothing of me remained but a mere nugget of consciousness. It felt as if some vast transcendent force was invading me without my volition, as if all the immanent good lying latent within me began to pour forth in a stream, to form a moving circle with the universal principle. Myself began to dissolve into the light that was like a great golden all-pervasive fog. It was a mystical moment of union with the mysterious infinite, with all things, all people.[12]

It is no surprise that the term most often used for the mystical experience in the East is *enlightenment*, a word that equates light with revelation. According to William Kaufman, in the Jewish tradition a bright light is a symbol of the presence of God. In the Zohar, a mystical commentary on the Bible, it is revealed that "at the center of the universe is an 'innermost light' of a brilliance beyond comprehension."[13] Even the word *Zohar* means "brightness" in Hebrew. At the time of Paul's illumination and conversion on the road to Damascus, "a light from heaven flashed about him" (Acts 9:3).

The first onset of this light for the mystic, accompanied as it usually is by revelation, is often the occasion for conversion to a spiritual life, though this does not necessarily include adherence to a particular doctrine or any organized religion, although that is often the case.

A mystical experience caused the conversion of Rulman Merswin, a wealthy, pious, and respected merchant of Strassburg in the fourteenth century. He was a student of Tauler, one of the great Catholic mystics, and had retired from his business to devote himself to spiritual growth. One day while strolling through his garden, his mind was filled with the image of the Cross, and "lifting his eyes to heaven he solemnly swore that he would utterly surrender his own will, person, and goods to the service of God."[14]

As we will see in a later chapter, the act of surrender of the personal will is often a catalyst for mystical perception. According to Evelyn Underhill's translation of Merswin's autobiography, this is what happened to him. "The reply [to his surrender] ... came quickly. A brilliant light shone about him: he heard in his ears a divine voice of adorable sweetness; he felt as if he were lifted from the ground .... Merswin's heart was filled by a new consciousness of the Divine."[15]

The light perceived by the mystic, however, is not always white or golden. Maurice Bucke, mentioned in Chapter Two, beheld a flame-colored cloud which accompanied his intellectual illumination. We remember the words of Teilhard de Chardin, quoted earlier, that "the world has little by little caught fire in my sight until, aflame all around me, it has become almost completely luminous from within." And Moses, of course, first perceived the Lord "in a flame of fire out of the midst of a burning bush" (Ex. 3:2).

Illustrated in this chapter are some of the most common aspects of the mystical experience: joy, beauty, peace, and light. There are other characteristics which are so crucial to understanding the mystic vision that they require a separate discussion. These are the perceptions of unity or the oneness of all creation; love as the predominate animating force of the universe; the sense of timelessness, or the "eternal now" of which the mystics speak; and the sense of knowing or certainty.

Relevant to our conclusion here, however, are the words that Blaise Pascal, a French philosopher, wrote after receiving a mystical illumination. They illustrate the ecstatic vision of the mystic—and of a mystic who truly awoke in heaven. These words were written on parchment containing a rough drawing of the Flaming Cross. It was found sewn up in Pascal's doublet upon his death.

> From about half past ten in the evening to
> about half an hour after midnight.
>   Fire.
> God of Abraham, God of Isaac, God of Jacob,
> Not the God of philosophers and scholars.
> Absolute Certainty: Beyond reason. Joy. Peace.
> Forgetfulness of the world and everything
>   but God.
> The world has not known thee, but I have
>   known thee.
>   Joy! joy! joy! tears of joy!

CHAPTER FOUR

The Beams of Love

The Experience of Love and Oneness

And we are put on earth a little space,
That we may learn to bear the beams of love.
                                  —William Blake

There is one Mind, one omnipresent Mind,
Omnific. His most holy name is Love....
              'Tis the sublime of man
Our noontide majesty, to know ourselves
Parts and proportions of one wondrous whole!
                        —Samuel Taylor Coleridge

Most of us have heard and even repeated the phrase "God is love" many times. But do we know what we mean by the words we so easily use? The mystics say they do. Most of us have also given lip service to the concept that we all are sisters and brothers, but have we actually experienced this oneness? The mystics claim they have.

These two concepts—the love of God and the love of humankind, the core of most major religions—are believed by most of us because we intuitively respond to what we feel should be true. Other people put aside spirituality because they see no evidence in their lives or in the world of the love and oneness in which they are told to believe. In the first line of his book *Divine Love and Wisdom*, Emanuel Swedenborg states, "Man knows that there is such a thing as love, but he does not know what love is."[1] Perhaps this is why the overwhelming certainty of a powerful, all-encompassing love, together with the actual experience of oneness with all creation, is the most emotionally uplifting experience that the mystics share.

The mystic seers often perceive through their revelations a cause-and-effect relationship between love and oneness, and this integrating force of love is often interpreted by them as the essence of God. In other words, "God is love" and that love animates God's whole creation. The physician Maurice Bucke, the writer F. C. Happold, and the priest-paleontologist Teilhard de Chardin each have had similar insights into the reality of love and oneness.

Bucke claimed that what we call love is the foundation principle of the world. Happold perceived love as a power working through creation. In an experience quoted earlier, he remarks that he was conscious "of a lovely, unexplainable pattern in the whole texture of things, a pattern of which everyone and everything was a part; and weaving the pattern was a Power; and that Power was what we faintly call Love." Teilhard de Chardin defined love as "an animating energy pulsating through the universe," and

" 'the supreme spiritual energy' linking all elements and persons in their 'irreplaceable and incommunicable essence' in a universal process of unification."[2]

It is fascinating to realize that the revelations of oneness experienced by the mystics is in accord with recent speculations in physics. Erwin Schroedinger, winner of the Nobel Prize in physics in 1933 for his contribution to wave mechanics, maintained "that all consciousness is essentially *one.*" Fritjof Capra, in *The Tao of Physics*, argues that one of the most important revelations of modern physics is an insight into the basic oneness of the universe. A deeper discussion of the similarities between mysticism and modern physics will continue in a later chapter on the nature of reality.

The following experiences show both the depth of the love that is discovered by the mystics and how love itself can be a catalyst for enlightenment.

British author Sir Francis Younghusband also had an insight that love is the foundation principle of the world. In *Heart of Nature*, he refers to his experience while contemplating the magnificence of the Himalayan mountains.

> I had a curious sense of being literally in love with the world. There is no other way in which I can express what I then felt. I felt as if I could hardly contain myself for the love which was bursting within me. It seemed as if the world itself were nothing but love ... At the back and foundation of things I was certain was love—and not merely placid benevolence, but active, fervent, devoted love, and nothing less. The whole world seemed in a blaze of love, and men's hearts were burning to be in touch with one another.[3]

The revelation that "God is love" came to a 14-year-old

girl in a strange manner. While attending a young people's religious meeting, she had an unexplainable, but imperative, inner urge to leave the service as it was ending and to go elsewhere in the church. She had the following experience:

> I have a vague memory of doors in all directions and finally of someone directing me upstairs. I didn't want to go upstairs, but not knowing where else to go, I went. I remember noting the dusty unwelcome appearance of the place as I climbed, until as I neared the top step something inexplicable happened. It was as though I had suddenly pushed up through the mists into a clear beautiful atmosphere. I neither saw nor heard. I just felt an indescribable ecstasy as I was suddenly conscious of an overwhelming love which seemed to encompass all that was and is and will be. It was all-encompassing and personal at the same time and lifted me to superb heights. I can remember feeling exultantly "This is God", and God, after all, was both personal and immense. I wish I had at my command the words which would truly convey the power, the depth, the infinity, the gentleness, the serenity and the intimacy which intermingled then. Somehow one doesn't separate the qualities which were evident. One just wants to enjoy the Oneness of it all.[4]

The following incident is important because it describes the revelation of love and oneness between a man and a group of complete strangers in an everyday setting:

> I was waiting for the train in a small waiting-

room of the railway station. About fifteen or twenty other people were gathered there for the same purpose, all total strangers to me. Some were sitting reading newspapers or talking, and others stood huddling about a stove in the corner of the room. There was the usual subdued chatter of voices with occasional laughter. It was a familiar, rather a common-place scene.

Suddenly, I was aware of some mysterious current of force, subtle, yet of unimagined potency, which seemed to sweep through that small drab waiting-room. A kind of glory descended upon the gathered company—or so it seemed to me. I looked at the faces of those around me and they seemed to be suffused with an inner radiance. I experienced in that moment a sense of profoundest kinship with each and every person there. I loved them all!— but with a kind of love I had never felt before. It was an all-embracing emotion, which bound us together indissolubly in a deep unity of being. I lost all sense of personal identity then. These people were no longer strangers to me. I *knew* them all. We were no longer separate individuals, each enclosed in his own private world, divided by all the barriers of social convention and personal exclusiveness. We were one with each other and with the Life which we all lived in common.[5]

The realization of great cosmic love is not only a product of the mystical experience, but is often a catalyst for the experience. The feeling and giving of selfless love can be a potent trigger for the beatific vision as it seems to take flight and return to the sender like a boomerang.

Jim Harrison was not at first glance a likely prospect for a mystical experience. He was a tobacco farmer in Zimbabwe and had flown reconnaissance missions in the Middle East and Italy during World War II. Although rarely a religious or contemplative thinker, one day he was questioning the probability of a God who would ignore the prayers of his wife who was in ill health. Ruminating on this, it occurred to him that perhaps it was a person's free will that caused his or her misfortunes. His train of thought then went as follows:

> Maybe it wasn't really God's fault after all! So then I thought all right, I take it all back, and filling my heart with the tender love often reserved for my little daughter, I projected it towards him, thinking, if you exist then I give you my love.
>
> ... I could feel this love being passed on and on, and then suddenly it returned—a brilliant shaft of light from out of the sky, brighter by far than the mid-morning sun, permeating me with such an intensity of happiness and Love as to halt me in my tracks with a jump for joy— and lingering for five or ten seconds before fading away. I knew intuitively that this light, plainly visible, extending into the sky, some- how, mysteriously, stemmed from within.
>
> So then I knew for certain that God does indeed exist, that he is love, that he is joy, that he is light, that he stems from within as much as from without, and that we alone are respon- sible for our own sufferings and problems in consequence of the mis-use of our free will.[6]

We are taught in 1 Corinthians 13 of the momentous power of love. "So faith, hope, love abide, these three; but the greatest of these is love" (1 Cor. 13:13). "Love never ends" (1 Cor. 13:8). Beautiful words, but merely words to most of us. However, there is evidence in the mystical experience that love does not fail, that if we open ourselves fully, letting go of our separate "ego-will," love will perform wonders in our lives. The following experience illustrates the healing power of love.

A young man was on a walk in the country with a young woman whom he loved and would later marry. She suffered from severe asthma, which was especially acute during times of exertion. As they climbed a hill, he felt quite desperate over her growing symptoms and his heart went out to her in empathy and love. The story continues in his words:

> We struggled on up the hill, and the next thing I noted was that the whole locality was illumined by an extraordinary, bright light. It was a cloudy and dull day and this extremely intense illumination did not appear to originate in any fixed centre, but was diffused equally throughout the entire terrain. Accompanying the light was a sense of the presence of an irresistible power wholly and utterly benevolent, and as far as I was concerned a feeling of complete happiness and well-being quite impossible to describe. The certainty of all-pervading and immutable love was so tremendous that I simply went on up the hill completely absorbed in this extraordinary experience and quite oblivious of the material surroundings. After an appreciable interval—I think a few minutes—the light gradually faded and I said to my companion, "Did you see that?"
>
> But she had noticed nothing unusual, and so the experience was obviously psychical and not

physical. However, she turned to me and said, "My asthma is all gone"—and this disease has never reappeared.[7]

The reader has probably observed that in the mystical experience the love and oneness that are revealed are not only for one's fellow human beings, but for all creatures. Indeed, if the mystics are correct, we humans are at home in a universe where we share kinship with all creation—animal, vegetable, and mineral. We remember Jacob Boehme's first illumination when a veil seemed lifted from nature and he saw that the grass and flowers were animated by a divine force that flowed through everything. A more modern mystic, Teilhard de Chardin, shared the same wisdom when he wrote, "Everything that is active, that moves or breathes, every physical, astral, or animate energy, every fragment of force, every spark of life, is equally sacred; for, in the humblest atom and the most brilliant star, in the lowest insect and the finest intelligence, there is the radiant smile and thrill of the *same Absolute*."[8]

The next story not only illustrates the essential unity of all life, but it is also a good example of another trigger of the mystical experience—strangely enough, despair. The person writing had been gravely ill. In his illness and general disillusionment with life, he found human beings essentially isolated from each other and life meaningless. He had, in fact, reached a state of giving up. We have heard that nature does not like a vacuum. In the following passages we observe how this "emptiness" was filled:

> On this particular day I wandered alone out to a meadow-like area and sat down against a pine. The day was beautiful and warm: the time shortly before noon ... I do not know how long I sat, but after a period of "empty" enjoyment, I

became intensely aware of many of the objects which were in the area. The rocks, the trees, the birds, the stream, the clouds, the flowers, became extremely meaningful to me. I realized the rocks, trees etc. were I; I they; all brothers. And I was exceedingly joyful in realizing this kinship....

Because of the experience I know that *everything* involved in this process is God, is Love, Light, Bliss ... that everything is in migration, movement, towards the Great Awakening to That which, in essence, every-thing is. Nothing, nothing is excluded from the "redemptive" process. Not only all men, but men and rocks and stars and trees are brothers, are divine, carry within them the splendour awakening to Itself.[9]

A similar experience is recounted by Brother Mandus in his autobiography, *This Wondrous Way of Life*. He recalls:

The greatest experience in my life ... when I was baptised by the Holy Spirit within. For one perfect second, unexpected, unheralded, and while I was doing a trivial task, my personal mind and body were fused in *Light*: a breathless unbearable *Light-Perfection*, as intense as the explosion of a flash of lightning within me ... In this timeless second I knew a Love, Knowledge and Ecstasy transcending anything I could understand or describe. I was lifted into the midst of God, in whom all people, all worlds, and every created life or thing moved and had their being.[10]

Bernadette Roberts, who shares her great spiritual quest

in her book *The Experience of No-Self: A Contemplative Journey*, describes a change of vision that began when she was camping in the Sierra Mountains. The vision change was a part of a longer extended mystical experience. "Gradually," she wrote, "I began to notice a shift in this seeing. Where at first it had been very nebulous and general, I soon noticed that when I visually focused in on a flower, an animal, another person, or any particular object, slowly the particularity would recede into a nebulous Oneness, so that the object's distinctness was lost to my mind."[11] It is not unusual among mystics who attain "the unitive life" to experience such a change in vision, while retaining the ability to focus in and out of everyday reality at will.

Elsewhere in her book, Roberts describes an exhilarating experience of oneness with nature which occurred while she was on a retreat with the Hermit Monks on the Big Sur.

> About the second day, toward late afternoon, I was standing on their windy hillside looking down over the ocean when a seagull came into view, gliding, dipping, playing with the wind. I watched it as I'd never watched anything before in my life. I almost seemed to be mesmerized; it was as if I was watching myself flying, for there was not the usual division between us. Yet, something more was there than just a lack of separateness, "something" truly beautiful and unknowable. Finally I turned my eyes to the pine-covered hills behind the monastery and still, there was no division, only something "there" that was flowing with and through every vista and particular object of vision. To see the Oneness of everything is like having special 3D glasses put before your eyes; I thought to myself: for sure, this is what they mean when they say

"God IS everywhere."[12]

Martin Buber, the famous Jewish theologian, had mystic sensitivities at a very early age. From his father, who managed a large estate, he learned respect for animals as well as people. He had a special awareness that enabled him to enter into deep relationships, not only with people but with all creatures.

In his autobiography, Buber described an affinity that he had with a horse belonging to his grandparents. One summer when he was eleven and visiting with his grandparents on their estate, he stole unobserved into the stable whenever possible and gently stroked the neck of "my darling, a broad dapple-gray horse." He goes on to relate:

> It was not a casual delight but a great, certainly friendly but also deeply stirring happening. If I am to explain it now, beginning from the still very fresh memory of my hand, I must say that what I experienced in touch with the animal was the Other, the immense Otherness of the Other, which, however, did not remain strange like the otherness of the ox and the ram, but rather let me draw near and touch it.... The horse, even when I had not begun by pouring oats for him into the manger, very gently raised his massive head, ears fliching, then snorted quickly, as a conspirator gives a signal meant to be recognizable only by his fellow conspirator; and I was approved.[13]

In his beautiful little book *Kinship With All Life*, J. Allen Boone relates his experience with the great German shepherd of movie fame, Strongheart. The mutual, intelligent, compassionate relationship that he established with Strongheart led him into an investigation of possible communication with other animals.

On the first night of his stay with Boone, there arose the problem of where Strongheart would sleep. He and Boone had different ideas. Strongheart, however, was able to communicate to Boone the reasoning behind his choice of sleeping arrangements. Thereafter, when Strongheart was long asleep, Boone was "wide awake with amazement." In the following, he relates his state of mind:

> I had spoken to Strongheart in my kind of language, a language of thoughts and feelings incased in human sound symbols. He had actually been able to receive and understand what I had said. Then he had answered me in his kind of language, a language made up of simple sounds and pantomime which he obviously felt I could follow without too much difficulty. Strongheart had understood me perfectly, and then with his keen and penetrating dog wisdom he had made it possible for me to understand him, too.[14]

It was obvious from his behavior that Strongheart was not only able to understand Boone's verbal language but was able to grasp his thoughts as well. When this became evident to Boone, he decided that this must be a reciprocal possibility. After a great deal of study and concentration, Boone was able to mentally communicate with Strongheart without outward means.

Astounded by this accomplishment and wanting to better understand it, Boone sought others who had developed this capacity. Ultimately, he did find them and was eventually able to communicate with many animals and insects, including worms and ants. He even made a special friend of a fly, which remained with him for an extended visit. The basic requirement for these experiences, he came to understand, was a complete change of attitude about the nature of the animal kingdom.

Another pioneer in animal-human relationships was Britain's Barbara Woodhouse, who had an intuitive understanding of human kinship with all creatures. In her autobiography, *Talking to Animals*, published in 1954, she recounts a lifetime of nurturing and training animals, especially horses, dogs, and farm animals. Her rapport and compassion won their love and loyalty. She was able to handle the most recalcitrant dogs and horses; her children were able to ride her heifers and even her bulls, so gentle had they become under her care. Woodhouse attributes her great ability to communicate with animals to her deep love and a lack of fear, which together create an atmosphere of mutual trust and regard.

Meister Eckhart, a Dominican of the fourteenth century, considered one of the most profound and erudite mystic theologians of all time, preached often about the equality and oneness of all creatures. He believed, according to Matthew Fox, a present-day Dominican following in his path, that "only a consciousness of our equality with all things results in authentic *gentleness* and *peace*."[15] In his sermons Eckhart has said: "The highest angel, the mind, and the gnat have an equal model in God," and "The greatest blessing in heaven and on earth is based on equality."[16]

There are great implications to the knowledge that we are one with all creation. Most importantly, we cannot isolate ourselves as superior beings and act with disregard for other life forms, as well as each other, without hurting ourselves in the bargain. Even if we consider humans first among equals, for just that reason we have great responsibility as stewards of life on our planet. As the Bible reports, we have been given "dominion" over God's creation, which God proclaimed "good" (Gen. 1:26, 31).

Such insight leaves us with an incredible opportunity. It is to discover and practice those actions that truly promote

the good of all. We are called to take ecological responsibility and work for balance in the natural order. What a
revelation to realize that what we perpetrate upon our
planet, our brothers and sisters, and our animal and
mineral cohabitants of the earth, we perpetrate upon
ourselves. When we war, we war with ourselves. When we
hate, we hate ourselves.

Most people, I believe, know these truths in their hearts,
but the revelations of the mystics make them unavoidable
and immediate. If love, as the mystical experience so
uniformly suggests, is the foundation principle of the
world, and we share the same holy life with all God's
creation, then we cannot avoid confronting the meaning
and consequences of our conduct.

The great poet and mystic of the seventeenth century,
John Donne, expressed the spiritual oneness and
interconnectedness of man's destiny in the following
passage from his essay "Meditation":

> No man is an island, entire of itself; every
> man is a piece of the continent, a part of the
> main; if a clod be washed away by the sea,
> Europe is the less, as well as if a promontory
> were, as well as if a manor of thy friends or of
> thine own were; any man's death diminishes
> me, because I am involved in mankind; and
> therefore never send to know for whom the bell
> tolls; it tolls for thee.

You Can See Forever

The Experience of Absolute Knowing

On a clear day
Rise and look around you
And you'll see who you are.
On a clear day
How it will astound you
That the glow of your being outshines ev'ry star.

You'll feel part of ev'ry mountain, sea and shore
You can hear from far and near
A world you've never heard before.
And on a clear day,
On that clear day
You can see forever and ever more.

—Alan Jay Lerner

"Swiftly arose and spread around me the peace and knowledge that pass all the argument of the earth," wrote Walt Whitman, in "Song of Myself." An unbelievable claim! Yet the mystics with virtually one voice say that in their moments of mystical union, they experience Truth: universal, all-encompassing Truth. Neither are they left after the experience with strengthened faith or belief, but absolute certainty. A verse from a poem by Frederic W. H. Myers forcefully illustrates the strength of their claims about the direct encounter of the presence of God.

> Whoso has felt the Spirit of the Highest
>   Cannot confound nor doubt Him nor deny:
> Yea, with one voice, O world, tho' thou
>   deniest,
>   Stand thou on that side, for on this am I.

Henry David Thoreau has also expressed in verse the bounty of mystical knowledge he received.

> I hearing get, who had but ears,
>   And sight, who had but eyes before;
> I moments live, who lived but years,
>   And truth discern, who knew but
>   learning's lore.
> I hear beyond the range of sound,
>   I see beyond the range of sight,
> New earths, and skies and seas around,
>   And in my day the sun doth pale his light.

And then, to make matters more difficult for the rest of us, the mystics claim that they cannot really convey these revelations of truth to us because they are ineffable and full of paradox. It is here that the communication of the mystics tends to break down, while the other aspects of the mystical experience such as joy, beauty, and love are more easily shared. Most of us upon hearing that someone had an experience of great joy and peace would not take exception; but when that person reveals that he or she dissolved into the undifferentiated unity and became one with the All and now knows the meaning of life, although he or she really can't explain it to us, we might be somewhat skeptical.

Our credibility is further strained when we learn that these experiences take place in an eternal now, outside of time as we experience it. Time and space, we are told, seem to be suspended, or perhaps are transcended, during the mystical experience.

"Let's forget the whole thing," might be our first reaction; "this material is too 'heady' for logical considera-tion." But before we give up, let's take a look at who these "oddball mystics" are. When we find that they are among the greatest creative minds and thinkers of all time, we might decide to tarry awhile and listen more closely. A compre-hensive list of these well-known people would take pages, but the caliber of it can be indicated by a few names chosen from the many possibilities.

If Ralph Waldo Emerson, T. S. Eliot, Johannes Brahms, Anwar Sadat, Dag Hammarskjöld, and Erwin Schroedinger are oddballs, then perhaps what we need in the world is more oddity. There are countless others whose reputations are just as great, many of whom I have already mentioned in the text. Just as important are the reports of the thousands of mystics whose names we might not recognize, but whose experiences attest to a reality undiscovered by most of us.

One definition of the mystical experience is that it is another way of knowing. Happold has described what happens in the mystical experience as an "extension of rational consciousness, resulting in an enlargement ... of perception."[1] Ken Wilber in his fascinating book *Quantum Questions* suggests that "in the mystical consciousness, Reality is apprehended directly and immediately ... subject and object become one in a timeless and spaceless act that is beyond any and all forms of mediation."[2]

Science has produced invaluable knowledge and will continue to do so. But many of the most brilliant scientists warn us that empirical data have limitations. They suggest that each of us, within our own consciousness, can open doors to perception. A remarkable number of physicists, while maintaining that the new insights provided by quantum physics in no way prove the validity of God or a spiritual reality, believe that they do remove obstacles to a reconciliation of science and religion. The following statements by Arthur Eddington in *Science and the Unseen World* convey the essence of these changes in scientific thinking and suggest that there is "another way" of knowing beyond the scientific method:

> Perhaps the most essential change is that we are no longer tempted to condemn the spiritual aspects of our nature as illusory because of their lack of concreteness. We have travelled far from the standpoint which identifies the real with the concrete.[3]
>
> Penetrating as deeply as we can by the methods of physical investigation into the nature of a human being we reach only symbolic description. Far from attempting to dogmatise as the nature of the reality thus symbolised, physics most strongly insists that its methods do not penetrate behind the symbolism. Surely then that mental and spiritual nature of ourselves, known in our minds by an intimate contact transcending the methods of physics, supplies just that interpretation of the symbols which science is admittedly unable to give.[4]

Erwin Schroedinger, the discoverer of "wave mechanics," speaks in the same vein as Eddington. "The scientific picture of the real world around me," he wrote, "is very deficient. It gives a lot of factual information, puts all our experience in a magnificently consistent order, but it is ghastly silent about all and sundry that is really near to our heart, that really matters to us."[5] In another essay, "The Oneness of Mind," he remarks, "We know, when God is experienced, this is an event as real as an immediate sense perception or as one's own personality."[6]

William James, renowned philosopher-psychologist of the late nineteenth and early twentieth centuries, included in his classic book *The Varieties of Religious Experience* a penetrating study of mysticism. His vast inquiries into the subject led him to the following conclusion. "Mystical experiences are as direct perceptions of fact for those who have them as any sensations ever were for us."[7] "Our normal waking consciousness ... is but one special type of consciousness, whilst all about it, parted from it by the filmiest of screens, there lie potential forms of consciousness entirely different.... No account of the universe in its totality can be final which leaves these other forms of consciousness quite disregarded."[8]

If we are persuaded to listen more closely to the tenets of mysticism due to the caliber of the minds that suggest its validity, our next question might be: What truths are revealed about the nature of reality during these special times of cosmic consciousness? Some we have already discussed: that a oneness or unity underlies and binds all creation; that love is the unifying force, the "foundation principle of the world." But there is much more about the nature of God and humankind, about heaven, hell, sin, time, space, and immortality that the mystics try to tell us— inhibited though they are by a language without words to convey the concepts they apprehend and the paradoxes they confront.

The very nature of the mystical experience is that the human creature has a direct experience of the Transcendent Reality, or God. However, for many mystics, the experience goes beyond contact to a union with this "ground of our being" in which the individual ego is embraced by a larger life. Arthur Koestler in cell 40, we recall, found that "the I had ceased to exist," and yet he felt "the experience was more real than any other experienced before." The South African schoolgirl Moyra Caldecott, when receiving communion, had a similar experience expressed in almost identical words. "I suddenly seemed to cease to be me (that is, in the sense of 'me' I had thought I was ...)." Claire Myers Owens, quoted in chapter 3, described her experience with similar words. "The ordinary 'I' ceased to exist. Nothing of me remained but a mere nugget of consciousness."

Tennyson, the nineteenth-century English poet, often had a similar experience in which the ego became part of a larger whole, and the loss of individual self was seen as a gain in a grander life. He describes it below:

> A kind of waking trance—this for lack of a
> better word—I have frequently had, quite up
> from boyhood, when I have been all alone.... all
> at once, as it were out of the intensity of the
> consciousness of individuality, individuality
> itself seemed to dissolve and fade away into
> boundless being, and this not a confused state
> but the clearest, the surest of the surest,
> utterly beyond words—where death was an
> almost laughable impossibility—the loss of
> personality (if so it were) seeming no
> extinction, but the only true life.[9]

In his book *Mysticism and Philosophy*, W. T. Stace deeply examined the self-transcending claims of the mystics. He studied numerous examples from different cultures, religions, and times, separating the language used to describe the experiences from the interpretations of the experience. He found the reports of the mystics consistent when they claimed to experience the self as "at once becoming one with or becoming dissolved in an infinite and universal self," while at the same time "the boundary walls of the separate self fade away, and the individual finds himself passing beyond himself and becoming merged in a boundless and universal consciousness."[10]

After approaching the subject with a great deal of skepticism, Stace reached the following conclusion:

> But if we have a very large number of such reports from independent sources all of which confirm the first report, our scepticism ought to abate somewhat. And if we find such independent reports coming from many diverse cultures, times, and countries of the world— from the ancient Hindus, from the medieval Christians, from Persians and Arabians, from Buddhist China, Japan, Burma, and Siam, from modern European and American intellectuals— this profoundly impressive agreement amounts to very strong evidence that the experiences were not misreported but were actually just what the mystics say they were.[11]

Four examples from various times and religions might serve to illustrate these claims of the possibility of union with the transcendent more vividly to the reader, remembering that we have already been introduced to them through Arthur Koestler, a modern intellectual, and Tennyson, a nineteenth-century poet.

The following passage is written in the ancient Hindu scripture, *The Upanishads*:

As a lump of salt thrown into water melts away ... even so, O Maitreyi, the individual soul, dissolved, is the Eternal—pure consciousness, infinite, transcendent. Individuality arises by the identification of the Self, through ignorance, with the elements; and with the disappearance of consciousness of the many, in divine illumination, it disappears.[12]

Al-Junayd, a Sufi mystic in A.D. 910, in describing this ultimate mystical experience uses similar words. "The saint ... is submerged in the ocean by unity, by passing away from himself.... He leaves behind him his own feelings and actions as he passes into the life with God."

Henry Suso, a Catholic mystic of the fourteenth century, gave this description:

When the spirit by the loss of its self-consciousness has in very truth established its abode in this glorious and dazzling obscurity, it is set free from every obstacle to union, and from its individual properties ... when it passes away into God.... In this merging of itself in God the spirit passes away.[13]

Martin Buber explained in his book *Ecstatic Confessions* that in these intense moments of mystical consciousness, "the soul experiences the ... unity of I and world; no longer a 'content,' but what is infinitely more than any content."[14] And in a later passage, he wrote, "The elementary notion in this mystery is a union ... with God. Ecstasy is originally an entering into God ... being filled with the god."[15]

In the last three examples, the mystics claim to have merged with God. This is not unusual. In fact, the most heavy charge mystics have borne through the ages is the accusation of pantheism, which is the philosophy that God is everything and everything is God. Religious mystics from both East and West have been tortured, put to death, and excommunicated because "higher authorities" in their respective religions have interpreted their communications about the knowledge gained from their enlightenment to be blasphemous. However, when the testimonies of mystics, again from both East and West, are looked at closely, we realize that this interpretation is largely due to the paradoxical nature of what they are trying to convey, and also because some statements are taken out of the context of their total revelations.

Yet when we compare teachings of the mystics, what they say is much more in accord with the similar yet importantly different doctrine called *panentheism*, which is the belief that God is *in* us and we are *in* God—that God is both immanent and transcendent. This concept could not be more beautifully expressed than in Ephesians 4:6: "[There is] one God and Father of us all, who is above all and through all and in all."

The idea of God being both immanent and transcendent is very simply stated by St. Augustine in his book *The Confessions:* "But Thou wert more inward to me, than my most inward part; and higher than my highest."[16]

God immanent is expressed beautifully by Erigena, the ninth-century Scottish mystic who said, "Every visible and invisible creature is a theophany or appearance of God." Nothing, however, could be a more precise description of immanence than Jesus' words in John 14:20: "I am in my Father, and you in me, and I in you." Also in the *Zohar*, as explained by Underhill, "God is considered as immanent in all that has been created or emanated, and yet is transcendent to all."[17]

In the last canto of *The Divine Comedy*, Dante describes his transcendent vision of the Supreme Reality, Who is so overwhelming and unspeakable that Dante prays he might have the power to translate his vision into words.

I saw that in its depths there are enclosed,
Bound up with love in one eternal book,
The scattered leaves of all the universe—
Substance, and accidents, and their relations,
As though together fused in such a way
That what I speak of is a single light.
The universal form of this commingling
I think I saw, for when I tell of it
I feel that I rejoice so much the more.

In this ultimate revelation of transcendence, Dante sees the Trinity and, finally, man himself. As Dante is enraptured by his vision of "a single semblance Within that Living Light ... / That semblance seemed to change." Dante then perceives within the whole "three rings / Of one dimension, yet of triple hue." Each seemed to be reflected from the one before. Within this Trinity, Dante finally perceives a human face. He wishes to comprehend how all were joined but is unable to through his own too feeble intellect. Understanding at last breaks through "by a lightning flash." Dante realizes that all is moved "By Love, which moves the sun and other stars."

In the West, we tend to think of the Trinity as an exclusively Christian concept, but that is inaccurate according to Bhagavan Das in *The Essential Unity of All Religions*. The whole of religion, the whole of philosophy, the whole of science is contained in the rule of three. "All the great religions," he claims, "describe this Ultimate Principle, either as Tri-Une, Trinity-in-Unity, Unity-in-Trinity, or as possessing three principal Attributes."[18] *

It is not uncommon for the mystic, especially the religious mystic who is seeking illumination, to be given the

*For a fuller exposition of this concept and the terms used for the Trinity in other major religions see discussion by Bhagavan Das in *The Essential Unity of All Religions*, p. 263.

supreme vision of the Trinity. St. Teresa of Avila, a well-known sixteenth-century mystic, recorded her experiences in *Interior Castle* with precision.

> By a representation of the truth in a particular way, the Most Holy Trinity reveals Itself, in all three Persons. First of all the spirit becomes enkindled and is illumined, as it were, by a cloud of the greatest brightness. It sees these three Persons, individually, and yet, by a wonderful kind of knowledge which is given to it, the soul realizes that most certainly and truly all these three Persons are one Substance and one Power and one Knowledge and one God alone.[19]

Not all revelations of the Trinity are given to religious saints, however. A fascinating insight into the Trinity came to Katharine Trevelyan, a modern English woman, which she revealed in her autobiography *Through Mine Own Eyes: The Autobiography of a Natural Mystic*. One evening she was musing thoughtfully about the concept of the Trinity, which she had never quite understood. She was sitting at an old, polished oak table on which there was a red candle and a plain crystal ball, a gift from her brother. Quite suddenly, she had the following revelation: "I noticed that the light from the candle falling through the crystal ball made the reflection of three flames on the polished table. I looked at them without thought and was enabled to see that just as there was only one candle on the table so there was only one God, the founder and ground of the whole universe—but for this earth (a speck in the Cosmos) the manifestation becomes split up, or threefold—even as the crystal ball made three reflected flames from one flame."[20]

Jacob Boehme, earlier quoted, claimed he had a vision of the Eternal Generation of the Holy Trinity. This view of the generation of the Trinity as an ongoing process is quite prominent in mystical literature. Jutzi Schultheiss, quoted from Elsbet Stagel's Sister-book of the Toss Convent, had a realization of the eternal generation of the Son by the Father and the oneness of all creation. "She ... recognized particularly how God is in all things and in all creatures.... She also saw clearly ... how the Son is eternally born from the Father, and that all the joy and bliss there is rests in the eternal birth."[21]

Meister Eckhart also taught from his mystical perception that the Father generates the Son in every human soul that is ready. He believed that when the will becomes one with the Father, the Son is born.

The communication problems of the mystics are most often caused by the paradoxical nature of what is revealed to them. We may be puzzled, as was Samuel Taylor Coleridge, by the claims of the mystics that God is one, yet He is also many. Coleridge is reported to have said, "I would make a pilgrimage to the deserts of Arabia to find the man who could make me understand how the *one can be many*." Each individual, according to the mystics, although experiencing life as a separate person, shares one life with God and all creation. Eckhart makes a fascinating analogy that may cast some light on an explanation. "Words flow forth," he says, "and yet remain within .... All creatures flow outward and nonetheless remain within."[22]

To make matters more puzzling, many mystics in their most intense moments of cosmic consciousness encounter what they call a void, which is also the fullness from which all flows. Stace calls this phenomenon the vacuum-plenum.

Below are some examples of these puzzling revelations. In the Hindu Scriptures it is written "That One, the Self, though never stirring, is swifter than thought.... Though standing still, it overtakes those who are running.... It stirs and it stirs not."[23]

The great Taoist mystic Lao-Tzu taught the following:

The Way [Tao] is like an empty vessel
That may yet be drawn from
Without ever needing to be filled.
It is bottomless: the very progenitor of all
    things in the world....
It is like a deep pool that never dries.
I do not know whose child it could be.
It looks as if it were prior to God.[24]

D. T. Suzuki, a modern teacher of Zen Buddhism, wrote of this phenomenon encountered in the mystical experience: "It is a state of absolute Suchness, of absolute Emptiness which is absolute fullness."[25]

Charles Fillmore, co-founder with Myrtle Fillmore of Unity School of Christianity, states the paradox in a slightly different way: "God is substance; but this does not mean matter, because matter is formed while God is the formless.... It is that which is the basis of all form yet enters not into any form of finality."[26]

Meister Eckhart postulates a possible solution to this paradox of the nature of God. He divides what he experienced into God and the Godhead. According to Eckhart, "God acts. The Godhead does not." The Godhead in Eckhart's definition sounds very much like what T. S. Eliot spoke of as "the still point of the turning world."[27]

It is also true that many mystics, even though they report the dissolution of the self, or the merging of the self into the greater whole, unmistakably feel the presence of a personality. Teilhard de Chardin, the Jesuit anthropologist mystic, writes of experiencing the Divinity as being infinite, yet personal. "The ocean that gathers up all the spiritual currents of the Universe is not only 'some-thing' but 'some-body.' And that somebody has a face and a heart."[28] It is interesting to note that the young girl quoted in Chapter Four had the same insights as that of the great Jesuit priest. "I can remember," she reported, "feeling exultantly 'This is

God,' and God, after all, was both personal and immense."[29]

Immanent and transcendent, the spirit of the God within responds to the grandeur of the God without. The mystics are privileged to know by direct experience—sometimes one and sometimes both. But most of us find it easier to acknowledge God Transcendent than God within our neighbors. The Hindus have a beautiful custom that keeps this reality before their minds. Upon meeting another, they clasp their hands together in front of their hearts and slightly bow their heads to acknowledge the divine spirit within the other person. In the following poem, Walt Whitman expresses his inner realization of the omnipresence of God.

> I see something of God each hour of the
>   twenty-four, and each moment then,
> In the faces of men and women I see God,
>   and in my own face in the glass,
> I find letters from God dropt in the street,
>   and every one is sign'd by God's name,
> And I leave them where they are, for I know
>   that wheresoe'er I go,
> Others will punctually come for ever and ever.

There are other messages about the nature of reality that the mystics have brought us. They appear full of paradox, but they are also full of hope. What the mystics reveal about time, eternity, and immortality will be the subject of the next chapter. However, the question of good and evil, the BIG question that so many of us wrestle with, belongs here with the revelations that God is everywhere manifest and that all that is real is holy and filled with the divine Presence. If so, whence evil and sin? The answer seems to be found in the question: What is *really real*?

If I interpret the mystics correctly, they are telling us that all of God's creation is good and all things work together for the good. The true God-created self is real and eternal. The separate ego is unreal and temporal. To the extent that we are attuned to and living from our divine Center, we are in "heaven," which is everywhere because God is manifest everywhere. To the extent that we are living in accordance with the dictates and fear of a separate ego, we are in hell, because hell is the sense of separation from God. Good is the essence of divine creation; evil and error are the products of the isolated, separated ego.

The following examples might serve to give the reader an idea of what is revealed in the mystical experience about good and evil and about heaven and hell. (It is important to note that not all mystical experiences come complete with revelations about all of these topics. The most pervasive realization, sometimes accompanied by more specifics, is simply that all is good and we can put our complete faith in reality.) The dramatic similarity of content and phrasing in these quotations is striking.

Error, Evil, Sin:

J. Redwood-Anderson (twentieth century): "The trouble begins when man asserts his peripheral position to be central: this is Original Sin."[30]

Abraham Isaac Kook (twentieth century): "When a person sins he has entered the world of fragmentation, and then every particular being stands by itself, and evil is evil in and of itself, and it is evil and destructive. When he repents out of love there at once shines on him the light from the world of unity, where everything is integrated into one whole, and *in the context of the whole there is no evil at all.*"[31] (Italics the author's.)

Aldous Huxley (twentieth century): "Sin is the manifestation of self. Men commit evil and suffer misery, because they are separate egos, caught in time."[32]

Arthur Osborn (twentieth century): "The evil of egoism is that of a peculiar blindness which causes a limited viewpoint to masquerade as though it were the Whole."[33]

Margaret Isherwood (twentieth century): "Sin might be defined as the failure to follow our own inner Light, as that way of thought or feeling that hinders our development, darkens our capacity for true insight, muddies our power of discrimination, and prevents us from going forward to fuller and happier awareness."[34]

Charles Fillmore (nineteenth into twentieth century): " 'Evil' represents error thought combinations; that part of consciousness which has lost sight of true principles and through sensation becomes enamored of the thing formed."[35]

Walt Whitman (nineteenth century): "And I say there is in fact no evil.... Clear and sweet is my soul, and clear and sweet is all that is not my soul." (from *Leaves of Grass*)

William Law (eighteenth century): "All errors are the want of love."[36] "Your own self is your own Cain that murders your own Abel. For every action and motion of self has the spirit of Anti-Christ and murders the divine life within you."[37]

William Blake (eighteenth century): "Error is created; truth is eternal."[38]

Meister Eckhart (thirteenth into fourteenth century): "The restlessness of all our storms comes entirely from self-will, whether we notice it or not." "To be in God is to experience an equanimity of joy regardless of pain and suffering."[39]

Heaven and Hell:

Meister Eckhart (thirteenth into fourteenth centuries): "Heaven has no appointed place. Neither does heaven stand within time, for its course is unbelievably swift."[40] "I say that in the kingdom of heaven everything is in everything else, and that everything is one, and that everything is ours."[41]

Jacob Boehme (sixteenth into seventeenth centuries): "There will never be any more heaven or hell than there is now. That soul hath heaven and hell in itself before, as it is written.... For behold the kingdom of God is within you."[42] "The true heaven is everywhere, even in that very place where thou standest and goest."[43]

Emanuel Swedenborg (eighteenth century): "Such persons [those who are opposed to love and wisdom] turn themselves backward from the Lord; and turning oneself backward is turning to hell."[44]

William Law (eighteenth century): "Men are not in hell because God is angry with them; they are in wrath and darkness because they have done to the light, which infinitely flows forth from God, as that man does to the light of the sun, who puts out his own eyes. " "No hell was made for them [mankind] ... they only stood in that state of division and separation from the Son and Holy Spirit of God, which by their own motion they had made for themselves."[45]

Charles Fillmore (nineteenth into twentieth century): "[The] one who is able to destroy both soul and body in Gehenna is the personal self or selfish ego that is in man."[46]

Myrtle Fillmore (nineteenth into twentieth century): "We should remember that man is always punished by his sins and not for them."[47]

Aldous Huxley (twentieth century): "Hell is total separation from God, and the devil is the will to that separation."[48]

Starr Daily (twentieth century): "When the mystical eyes are opened the Kingdom of Heaven is experienced." "In my mystical experience, all this [experience of hell on earth in prison] was reversed.... His infinite love and goodness was all that had any existence. Joyousness and tranquility were so vast that they were almost beyond physical endurance. What had been hell on earth became heaven on earth—the only reality."[49]

Jae Jah Noh (twentieth century): "Spiritual work commences when one realizes he is in hell, and that he does not have to be."[50]

Those who have had mystical experiences feel compelled to speak because they have found that we are in fact borne up in the "everlasting arms" of a benign universe. They have found light and would not have others walk in darkness. Three examples might best serve to illustrate the character of the reality that is often revealed to the mystic. Two are taken from experiences already quoted: Maurice Bucke and F. C. Happold in Chapter Two; the third is a continuation of the experience of Claire Myers Owens quoted in Chapter Three.

Maurice Bucke, quoted earlier, speaking of his own

experience of intellectual illumination wrote the following: "Among other things he did not come to believe, he saw and knew that the Cosmos is not dead matter but a living Presence, that the soul of man is immortal, that the universe is so built and ordered that without any peradventure all things work together for the good of each and all, that the foundation principle of the world is what we call love and that the happiness of everyone is in the long run absolutely certain."[51]

F. C. Happold discovered the same reality. "I was conscious of a lovely, unexplainable pattern in the whole texture of things ... and weaving the pattern was a Power; and that Power was what we faintly call Love. I realized that we are not lonely atoms in a cold, unfriendly, indifferent universe, but that each of us is linked up in a rhythm ... to which we can submit ourselves trustfully and unreservedly."[52]

Only a small part of the luminous and extensive experience of Claire Myers Owens, the despondent housewife, was reported in Chapter Three. The following paragraph, excerpted from the complete account, is much in accord with what we have already heard.

> Extraordinary intuitive insights flashed across my mind. I seemed to comprehend the nature of things. I understood that the scheme of the universe was good, it was only man that was out of harmony with it. I was inherently good, not evil as our Western society had taught me as a child; all people were intrinsically good. Neither time nor space existed on this plane. I saw into the past and observed man's endless struggle toward the light. Love and suffering and compassion for the whole human race so suffused me that I knew I never again could condemn any person no matter

what he or she did. I also saw into the distant
future and beheld man awakening gradually to
the good in himself, in others, moving with
the harmonious rhythm of the universe,
creating a new golden age—in some sweet
tomorrow.[53]

Very legitimately, the reader might doubt whether this
kind of optimism could stand up to the cruelty and horror
that we know exists in the world. The best answer the
author can give is a verse from Emerson; the words of
Evelyn Underhill, perhaps the most thorough student of
mysticism whose work has appeared in print; and an
experience of a young Jewish woman during the holocaust.
All were mystics.

'Tis not in the high stars alone,
Nor in the cup of budding flowers,
Nor in the red-breast's mellow tone,
Nor in the bow that smiles in showers,
But in the mud and scum of things
There alway, alway something sings.

The following words were written by Underhill as a
preface to her book *Practical Mysticism*, going to print just
as Britain was entering the first world war. "That deep
conviction of the dependence of all human worth upon
eternal values, the immanence of the Divine Spirit within
the human soul, which lies at the root of a mystical
concept of life, is hard indeed to reconcile with much of
the human history now being poured red-hot from the
cauldron of war." However, she goes on to say, " 'Practical'
mysticism means nothing if the attitude and the discipline
which it recommends be adapted to fair weather alone."
She continues:

It is significant that many of these [mystical] experiences are reported to us from periods of war and distress: that the stronger the forces of destruction appeared, the more intense grew the spiritual vision which opposed them. We learn from these records that the mystical consciousness has the power of lifting those who possess it to a plane of reality which no struggle, no cruelty, can disturb: of conferring a certitude which no catastrophe can wreck. Yet it does not wrap its initiates in a selfish and other-worldly calm, isolate them from the pain and effort of the common life. Rather, it gives them renewed vitality; administering to the human spirit not—as some suppose—a soothing draught, but the most powerful of stimulants.[54]

Etty Hillesum, in her posthumously printed diary, described as "a testimony of faith, hope and love, written in hell," reinforces the argument of Evelyn Underhill. A native of Holland during the holocaust, Etty, 29 years old at the time of her death at Auschwitz, went voluntarily to the concentration camp to be a comfort to her people and share their fate. The following are a few brief excerpts from the diary she was able to smuggle out before her final journey to Auschwitz.

> You know, if you don't have the inner strength while you're here to understand that all outer appearances are a passing show, as nothing beside the great splendour (I can't think of a better word right now) inside us— then things can look very black here indeed....
> The misery here is quite terrible and yet, late at night when the day has slunk away into

the depths behind me, I often walk with a spring in my step along the barbed wire and then time and again it soars straight from my heart—I can't help it, that's just the way it is, like some elementary force—the feeling that life is glorious and magnificent, and that one day we shall be building a whole new world.[55]

Etty Hillesum, of the twentieth century, shared the same revelation as Julian of Norwich of the fourteenth century: "All shall be well, and all manner of things shall be well."

The Image of Eternity

The Experience of Immortality

With wide-embracing love
Thy Spirit animates eternal years,
Pervades and broods above,
Changes, sustains, dissolves, creates and rears.

Though earth and man were gone,
And suns and universes ceased to be,
And Thou were left alone,
Every existence would exist in Thee.

There is not room for Death
Nor atom that his might could render void:
Thou—THOU art Being and Breath,
And what THOU art may never be destroyed.
                                        —Emily Brontë

Time is the image of eternity.
                    —Plato

In the words of Madame Guyon, a French mystic of the turn of the eighteenth century:

> When my spirit had been enlightened, my soul was placed in an infinite wideness.... Past, present, and future are there in the manner of a present and eternal moment, not as prophecy, which regards the future as a thing that is to come, but as everything is seen in the present in the eternal moment, in God himself; without knowing how one sees or knows it.[1]

The following was written by Arthur W. Osborn, a twentieth-century mystic. "Eternity exists at every moment on the time plane. It is Here-Now just as much as at any future time."[2] Both Guyon and Osborn echo Meister Eckhart of the thirteenth century, who taught that: "There [in eternity] you have in a present vision everything which ever happened or ever will happen. There is no before or after, there in eternity; everything is present and in this ever-present vision I possess everything."[3]

The enigma of time and space is present in the writings of both the mystic and the scientist. Consider the following statements by prominent physicists.

Erwin Schroedinger ended his essay entitled "The Mystic Vision" with the following words, "For eternally and always there is only *now*, one and the same now; the present is the only thing that has no end."[4] Scientist J. G. Whitrow explained that in the world view fostered by relativity theory, "external events permanently exist and we merely come across them."[5] Max Planck wrote the following about the concept of space:

> In modern mechanics ... it is impossible to obtain an adequate version of the laws for which we are looking, unless the physical

system is regarded *as a whole.* According to modern mechanics [field theory], each individual particle of the system, in a certain sense, at any one time, exists simultaneously in every part of the space occupied by the system.[6]

Science fiction has accustomed us somewhat to goings to and fro in space/time, but when we seriously try to understand these concepts using the linear thinking and symbols that we have available, most of us end up frustrated. The mystics experience the same enormous frustration when they attempt to communicate, within the framework of our language, what they have apprehended, as do we when we try to understand it. There is a huge disparity between the mystic's unspeakable experience and the language which is available to express it. For this reason, the most articulate mystics turn to poetry and to poetic symbolism to suggest the inexpressible.

Honoré de Balzac explained much of his mystical philosophy in a poetic metaphysical treatise, lightly disguised as a novel. As Seraphita, the main character, prepares for her final transition to the spiritual realm through her physical death, she instructs her two friends (disciples) in the beneficence of infused prayer or, in other words, prayer that leads to a mystical knowing:

> You acquire alacrity of spirit; in one instant you can be present in every region; you are borne, like the Word itself, from one end of the world to the other. There is a harmony—you join in it; there is a light—you see it; there is a melody—its echo is in you. In that frame you will feel your intellect expanding, growing, and its insight reaching to prodigious distances; in fact, to the spirit, time and space are not.[7]

Johannes Anker-Larsen, a Danish novelist born in 1874, experienced moments of mystical awareness from his childhood on. Through the years he became aware of the ephemeral nature of time and space. "In the everlasting Now," he wrote, "there is neither Space nor Time, neither limitation nor distinction. Even the language of the gods would be inadequate to describe it, and the 'language of Heaven' cannot be spoken or written; it is *lived*." In the following passage, he describes, as best he is able, "a summer day's meeting between Time and Eternity":

I had been sitting in the garden working and had just finished. That afternoon I was to go to Copenhagen, but it was still an hour and a half before the departure of the train. The weather was beautiful, the air clear and pure. I lighted a cigar and sat down in one of the easy-chairs in front of the house. It was still and peaceful— around me and within me. Too good, in fact, to allow one to think much about anything. I just sat there. Then it began to come, that infinite tenderness, which is purer and deeper than that of lovers, or of a father toward his child. It was in me, but it also came to me, as the air came to my lungs. As usual, the breathing became sober and reverent, became, as it were, incorporeal; I inhaled the tenderness. Needless to say the cigar went out. I did not cast it away like a sin, I simply had no use for it.

This deep tenderness which I felt, first within myself and then even stronger around and above me, extended further and further—it became all-present. I saw it, and it developed into knowing, into knowing all, at the same time it became power, omnipotence, and drew me into the eternal Now.

That was my first actual meeting with Reality; because such is the real life: a Now which *is* and a Now which *happens*. There is no beginning and no end. I cannot say any more about this Now. I sat in my garden, but there was no place in the world where I was not.[8]

The space/time that most of us experience as substantial has an illusory nature to mystical perception. Scenes disintegrate and reform, and what seems real becomes only apparent. Although not a necessary part of the mystical experience, this "fantastic" dissipation of space/time into "other" places and "other" times happens often to mystics. Loren Hurnscot told of one such experience. This occurrence is particularly fascinating because it was experienced by two people simultaneously.

The highlight of my visit, and one of the occasions of our lives, came on New Year's Eve. Alison and I went by a variety of buses to Ripon, and set off on a cloudy winter after- noon, in a taxi, to the gates of Fountains Abbey. I had clamoured for years to revisit it, for I had loved it as a child and had never seen it since. We dismissed the taxi at the gates, walked by frost-whitened paths between silvery evergreens, then down towards the roar of the Skell and the dim lovely ruins. Repair-work was going on and scaffolding towered above the Chapel of the Nine Altars. As dusk fell, we stood together on the south side of the cloister- garth, looking north, towards the cedar and the great grass-grown walls and the tower. And as we stood silently watching, they began to change. A soft, silvery-amber and quite unearthly light like warm moonlight lay over them. But there was no moon; it was not due to rise for hours yet. In utter silence—where was the roar of the Skell?—the whole ruin changed, rebuilt itself: the walls were intact, the church and the Chapel of the Nine Altars became roofed and perfect. The pinnacled tower stood out newly finished, a deeper amber than the rest. The entire structure was silver-gilt in colour, and this colour seemed to be struck out of it by the silvery light in which it was bathed. We both stood awestruck, wordless, not moving, for what seemed a long time. "There's no scaffolding," breathed Alison at last in a soft amazed tone. I didn't answer, for I thought, "Why should there be scaffolding? We're seeing it as it was about 1520.[9]

One of the greatest mystics of modern times, Katharine Trevelyan, an Englishwoman, was compelled to live in Germany with her German husband and child during the years preceding World War II. She was extremely sensitive to the foreboding and impending evil that was then gripping Germany. In her book *Through Mine Own Eyes*, she told of a time-shattering experience.

I came back from shopping one day carrying a basket, down the main street with its streetcars, cobbles, and modern houses with patterns made on their facades by their red brick. A brigade of young German soldiers, all in gray, came marching from their barracks into the center of the town.... I was not thinking about the soldiers, but looked up absent-mindedly at them as they passed. To my horror, I saw they were all dead, and yet they were moving down the street as though they were living men. I saw their sunken eyes, their fallen-in faces, the clammy pallor, their teeth showing in the grin of death. Their death seemed death to me also; I was gripped by their cold, their nothingness. Then I shook myself free again, and they changed before my eyes. True, they were gray and somber; true, they were sad and most deeply unlike God's picture of young men in their early twenties, but alive they certainly were in a dim and stagnant sort of way. What I had seen, when they so clearly were marching corpses, I do not know to this day.[10]

Katharine Trevelyan had been a mystic her whole life, but the following experience was a culmination of all those which had preceded. It is an example not only of the illusory nature of time and space, but also of the gifts of knowledge, joy, and beauty that come with the Beatific Vision.

When I knew myself nothing but a prize fool in love, I took my pain and foolishness in both hands and quite simply offered them to God, whom I recognized through this last anguish to be the backcloth of my life and my eternal love.

What followed was beyond me to understand....

It felt as though an infinitely complex machine had in all its parts, between one moment and the next, clicked silently into gear and started to work with inexorable power.

I saw face to face at last.

Light streamed down from the sky such as I have never beheld. The sun shone with a new light, as though translucent gold were at its heart. I saw not only the physical sun but the spiritual sun also, which poured down on me as I walked in the garden at Coombe.

The wonder was beyond anything I have ever read or imagined or heard men speak about. I was Adam walking alone in the first Paradise. That it was a garden near the outskirts of London in the twentieth century made no difference, for time was not, or had come round again in a full circle. Though I was Adam, I had no need of Eve, for both combined within me. Marriage and maternity fulfilled and surpassed, I had run beyond womanhood and become a human being.

Every flower spoke to me, every spider wove a miracle of intricacy for my eyes, every bird understood that here was Heaven come to earth....

But there was something more wonderful than the Light within the light—more wonderful than the standstill of time. It was that God walked with me in the garden as He did before the Fall. Whether I sat, whether I walked, He was there—radiant, burningly pure, holy beyond holy.

When I breathed, I breathed Him; when I asked a question He both asked and answered it.

My heart was unshuttered to Him and He came and went at will; my head had no limit or boundary of skull, but the Spirit of God played on me as though my mind were a harp which reached the zenith.

Every prayer was fulfilled, every possible desire for the whole world consummated; for

His Kingdom had come and I had beheld it with
my very eyes.[11]

If space and time are "contained" in an eternal now, it
follows that all life existing in space and time is also a part
of an eternal now. It is not surprising then that the
revelation of humanity's immortality is central to the
mystical experience. We recall that Tennyson, during his
enlightenment, perceived death as "an almost laughable
impossibility."

Symeon, a Greek theologian and mystic of the tenth
century, expressed in his "Love Songs to God" the following
realization: "I who am mortal and an insignificant person in
the world, behold the entire Creator of the world in myself;
and even while I live, I embrace all blossoming life in
myself and know that I shall not die."[12]

Many mystics perceive, however, not only immortality
but evolution as the future for the human spirit. In his
novel of the same name, Balzac has Seraphita explain to her
disciple, Minna, that "men are constantly mistaken in their
science, not seeing that everything on their globe is relative
and subordinate to a general cycle, an incessant productive-
ness which inevitably involves progress, and an aim. Man
himself is not the final creation; if he were, God would not
exist."[13]

Jalal-uddin Rumi, the Sufi mystic poet, expressed a
similar idea in the following poem:

I died a mineral, and became a plant.
I died a plant and rose an animal.
I died an animal and I was man.
Why should I fear? When was I less by dying?
Yet once more I shall die as man, to soar
With the blessed angels; but even from
        angelhood
I must pass on. All except God perishes.

When I have sacrificed my angel soul,
I shall become that which no mind ever
    conceived.
O, let me not exist! for Non-Existence
    proclaims,
"To Him we shall return."

Teilhard de Chardin, a mystic and prophet of the future, described life as a rise in consciousness and believed that humankind is evolving toward a *super-life.* "We have said," Teilhard wrote, "that life, by its very structure, having once been lifted to its stage of thought, cannot go on at all without requiring to ascend even higher."[14]

Aldous Huxley, author of *The Perennial Philosophy*, puts forth the premise that there is a difference between immortality and survival. "Immortality," he asserts, "is participation in the eternal now of the divine Ground; survival is persistence in one of the forms of time. Immortality is the result of total deliverance."[15] This theory seems to be compatible with the evolution of the human spirit and suggests that the soul would progress from mere survival to immortality.

Aldous Huxley's "Minimum Working Hypothesis" is a cogent summing up of a discussion of the nature of reality as revealed through the mystical experience. In keeping with his comprehensive study of mystics from the major religions and cultures through time, he uses language from various religious orientations. His hypothesis concludes:

That there is a Godhead, Ground, Brahman, Clear Light of the Void, which is the unmanifested principle of all manifestations.
That the Ground is at once transcendent and immanent.
That it is possible for human beings to love, know and, from virtually to become

actually identical with the divine Ground.

That to achieve this unitive knowledge of the Godhead is the final end and purpose of human existence.

That there is a Law or Dharma which must be obeyed, a Tao or Way which must be followed, if men are to achieve their final end.

That the more there is of self, the less there is of the Godhead; and that the Tao is therefore a way of humility and love, the Dharma a living law of ... self-transcending awareness."[16]

Of "the way," we shall learn more in the next chapter.

SEVEN

Wake Up
This Morning

Activators of the
Mystical Experience

Run to his feet—
he is standing close to your head right now.
You have slept for millions and millions of years.
Why not wake up this morning?

                                        —Kabir

That Light whose smile kindles the Universe,
That Beauty in which all things work and move,
That Benediction which the eclipsing Curse
Of birth can quench not, that sustaining Love
Which through the web of being blindly wove
By man and beast and earth and air and sea,
Burns bright or dim, as each are mirrors of
The fire for which all thirst.

                                        —Shelley

Who can aspire to being a mystic? Why does it seem that one person is chosen over another to be given this grace? We have read in the Bible, "many are called, but few are chosen" (Mt. 22:14). This is also true for the wondrous journey to make "an exploration into God." The "chooser," however, is the individual self, for the path is open to all. In each soul lies the potential for union with God, or the Divine Transcendent Reality, but, as Eckhart has stated, it is covered by "thirty or forty skins or hides, just like an ox's or a bear's, so thick and hard." Nevertheless, claim Eckhart and other mystics, this "divine spark" remains pure, incorruptible, and holy.

Raynor Johnson, a mystic as well as student and teacher of mystical religion, claims in his book *Watcher on the Hills* that "there is a centre in the soul which can relate itself in mystical experience directly and immediately to that which lies behind appearance."[1] F. C. Happold, also a mystic and scholar, agrees. "Men possess," he wrote, "an organ or faculty which is capable of discerning spiritual truth, and, in its own spheres, this faculty is as much to be relied on as are other organs of sensation in theirs."[2]

One of the most acclaimed modern mystics and teachers, Joel Goldsmith in *A Parenthesis in Eternity* speaks of this center as a bud ready to open at the appropriate time. "Within the consciousness of each one of us there is a something. It is impossible to reveal the true nature of it, except to explain that to me it seems as if it were a tightly closed bud, almost like a fresh new rosebud. As students come to me, I can sometimes feel that something in them, that tight little bud in their consciousness, and I know it is their spiritual nature, the Christ or the divinity of them."[3]

When this bud opens, or the "center" is activated, is largely up to us. We, however, are caught up in our material lives, "getting and spending," and in our individual egos, unable to let go of our separate selves. "God is at home in us," suggests Eckhart, "but we are abroad." A beautiful passage from *A Parenthesis in Eternity* is an affirmation of the need for surrender.

> There is a Spirit of Christ [Goldsmith uses the term *Christ* to mean the spirit of God], and It will raise up our mortal bodies; It will be the bread and the wine and the water to our experience; It will take us out of those empty years of the locusts. There is a Spirit, but there is a price to be paid for It—a surrender. Spirituality cannot be added to a vessel already full of materiality. We cannot add the kingdom of heaven to our personal sense of self; we cannot attain the kingdom of heaven if there is an inordinate love of personal power, a love of glory, a love of name or fame, or a desire merely to show forth the benefits and the fruitage of the Spirit in the form of better human circumstances. Our vessel must be empty of self before it can be filled with the grace of God."[4]

Francis Thompson relates similar wisdom in his poem "In No Strange Land."

> The angels keep their ancient places;—
> Turn but a stone and start a wing!
> 'Tis ye, 'tis your estranged faces,
> That miss the many-splendored thing.

Enlightenment is compared by many mystics to awakening from a dream, from illusions that we have created in our separation from God. A clear example of such awakening would be that of Saul on the way to Damascus, and even he retired from the world for a space of time before he was able to integrate the experience and activate this new Reality in his life, as Paul.

In our journey toward God realization, a mystical experience is a grace—a light thrown upon our path, an intimation of the divine reality that will be our dwelling place when we have put off our "forty skins" and have accepted our spiritual heritage. It can serve as a beacon to lead us forward into a richer life in which faith and increased spiritual understanding will be our guides to further growth, or it can catapult us into a quest that will not be satisfied until we reach the goal of living continually in the divine Presence.

Although the mystical experience is a grace and cannot be commanded, it can be prepared for, either consciously or unconsciously. Life itself has a way of preparing us by continuously leading us to dead ends in the material world where we originally seek our fortunes. Our egos bruised and sore, we become open to new possibilities of being. The mystic path or way, which is essentially the same in the East and West, is available to all who are ready to push ahead consciously on their spiritual journey. The way is difficult, but those who have reached this "promised land" assure us that the reward is the "pearl of great price." The path ultimately leads away from our separate self, our demanding ego, into the hands of a loving God.

Arthur Osborn defines egoism, the focus of the separate self, as "a narrowing of the circle of attention, thus creating a 'spot-light' of consciousness with apparently separate interests"—a blindness which "causes a limited viewpoint to masquerade as though it were the Whole."[5] In some circumstances, though, certain triggers or catalysts can work to cause, however momentarily, a cessation of the ego consciousness and allow the Whole or God consciousness to be experienced. "As human beings," wrote Joel Goldsmith, "we are in the tomb where the Christ lies buried, and all that the world sees is this living corpse in which we are entombed. Within us, in this tomb of human selfhood, is the

Christ, and in certain moments of our lives, such as can happen to us this moment, an experience takes place, and then a few hours later when we look in the mirror, we suddenly find that our eyes have been opened."[6]

Andrew Greeley, a Catholic priest, sociologist, and prolific author, has done extensive research on the mystical experience and mystical consciousness. In his book *Ecstasy: A Way of Knowing*, Father Greeley includes a discussion on the triggers of mystical experience. He suggests that these things serve to distract the sentinel ego from its watch over our separateness.

> The triggers of the ecstatic experience can be viewed as signals which remind the person of his co-naturality with the universe. A splendid crash of sound in a symphony, a rose-colored cloudbank hanging over a lake at sunset, the misty quiet of a stained-glass cathedral ... the stars set in the night-sky canopy, a particularly pleasurable experience of lovemaking—all of these remind the human that the universe of which he is a part is overwhelming, and in fact overwhelmingly gracious. Triggers sweep away the distractions, the troubles, the anxieties, even the activities of the rational world, and leave man temporarily passive in the grip of Being and hence predisposed to experience, albeit transiently, the power of Being revealed totally and directly.[7]

In past chapters, we have already discussed and illustrated several of the catalysts for the mystical experience such as the beauties of nature, great love, and despair. However, there are many others. The following list encompasses the better known triggers: great beauty such as in nature and art; ego-transcending love; despair; pain and illness; artistic works such as poetry, music, literature, and art; religion—religious writings, services, and places; creative work; sexual love; childbirth; an attitude of deep questioning; isolation, especially in combination with the attitude of questioning; a teacher; meditation and contemplation; and the following of the mystic path.

Occasionally circumstances produce several catalysts that work together to trigger the mystical experience. Such was the case of Ignatius of Loyola in fifteenth-century Spain. As a younger son of minor nobility, Ignatius was known as a rake and a womanizer who sought his future as a soldier in the service of a powerful local nobleman. In a skirmish defending a castle, he was severely wounded and required a very painful operation: a bone was sawed and reconstructed without any anesthetic. While recovering in his family castle, Ignatius requested chivalric romances to read. However, none could be found, so he was given books on religion and the lives of the saints. It was after this that he began having the life-transforming mystical experiences that led eventually to the foundation of one of the great religious orders, the Jesuits, and to his own journey toward becoming one of the mystics who has achieved "the unitive life."

Margaret Prescott Montague, novelist, short-story writer, and poet, suffered progressive blindness as a child and later became almost totally deaf. At one point in her life, she was recovering from surgery that involved physical pain and, later, acute mental depression. During that time she had an experience in which she claimed, "my eyes were opened, and for the first time in all my life I caught a glimpse of the ecstatic beauty of reality."[8]

One cloudy day Margaret had been wheeled out on the porch where patients enjoyed the air and met with visitors. A wind was blowing, but other than that, it was a very ordinary day. Here is her account of the experience that followed:

I cannot now recall whether the revelation came suddenly or gradually; I only remember finding myself in the very midst of those wonderful moments, beholding life for the first time in all its young intoxication of loveliness, in its unspeakable joy, beauty, and importance. I cannot say exactly what the mysterious change was. I saw no new thing, but I saw all the usual things in a miraculous new light—in what I believe is their true light. I saw for the first time how wildly beautiful and joyous, beyond any words of mine to describe, is the whole of life. Every human being moving across that porch, every sparrow that flew, every branch tossing in the wind, was caught in and was a part of the whole mad ecstasy of loveliness, of joy, of importance, of intoxication of life.

It was not that for a few keyed-up moments I *imagined* all existence as beautiful, but that my inner vision was cleared to the truth so that I *saw* the actual loveliness which is always there, but which we so rarely perceive; and I knew that every man, woman, bird, and tree, every living thing before me, was extravagantly beautiful, and extravagantly important. And, as I beheld, my heart melted out of me in a rapture of love and delight....

Once out of all the gray days of my life I have looked into the heart of reality; I have witnessed the truth; I have seen life as it really is—ravishingly, ecstatically, madly beautiful, and filled to overflowing with a wild joy, and a value unspeakable. For those glorified moments I was in love with every living thing before me—the trees in the wind, the little

birds flying, the nurses, the internes, the
people who came and went. There was nothing
that was alive that was not a miracle. Just to
be alive was in itself a miracle. My very soul
flowed out of me in a great joy.[9]

Works of art rank next to nature as the most usual
catalyst for the mystical experience. This should not be
surprising since many artists, even if they are not "full-
fledged mystics," share the mystical temperament. After
her extensive studies of mysticism, Evelyn Underhill
concluded that all real artists are sharers, to some degree,
in the Illuminated Life. Some artists very consciously
pursue the communication of the mystic vision, as did
William Blake, who was a fully illumined mystic. Blake
believed that it was his vocation to bring this mystical
illumination—this heightened vision of reality—to the
consciousness of ordinary men and to cleanse the doors of
perception of the race. In the following excerpt from his
poem "Jerusalem," he explains this mission:

... I rest not upon my great task
To open the Eternal Worlds, to open the
    immortal Eyes
Of Man inwards into the Worlds of Thought:
    into Eternity
Ever expanding in the Bosom of God, the
    Human Imagination.
O Saviour, pour upon me thy Spirit of
    meekness and love,
Annihilate the Selfhood in me: be thou all my
    life.

The profound impact that literature of a mystical
nature can have was illustrated in Chapter Two by Maurice
Bucke, whose dramatic experience came after reading with

friends the works of the poets Wordsworth, Whitman, Shelley, and others.

The beauty of music, the "international language," also speaks directly to the soul and is not only a source of great inspiration but is often a catalyst for the mystical experience. "The mystery of music," writes Evelyn Underhill, "is seldom realized by those who so easily accept its gifts. Yet of all the arts music alone shares with great mystical literature the power of waking in us a response to the life-movement of the universe: brings us— we know not how—news of its exultant passions and its incomparable peace. Beethoven heard the very voice of Reality, and little of it escaped when he translated it for our ears."[10]

Many great musicians and composers are also mystics and are able to tap into transcendent sources of inspiration. A charming book, *Talks With Great Composers* by Arthur Abell, reports intimate conversations with some of the great musical masters in which they confide their mystical approach to music.

Joseph Joachim, a famous violinist of his time, arranged a meeting between Arthur Abell and Johannes Brahms because of his interest in Abell's plan to write a book about genius and inspiration. During their extensive conversation, Brahms confided that he believed all truly inspired ideas come from God, and revealed the secrets of how he composed, moved by the soul forces within him. "Spirit is the light of the soul," Brahms said. "Spirit is universal. Spirit is the creative energy of the Cosmos. The soul of man is not conscious of its powers until it is enlightened by Spirit. Therefore, to evolve and grow, man must learn how to use and develop his own soul forces."[11]

When asked how he contacted these divine omnipotent powers, Brahms stated that he always contemplated the passage from John "I and the Father are one" (Jn. 10:30) before beginning his work. He then asked three important questions—whence? wherefore? and whither?—after which he explained,

> I immediately feel vibrations that thrill my whole being.... These are the Spirit illuminating the soul-power within, and in this exalted state, I see clearly what is obscure in my ordinary moods; then I feel capable of drawing inspiration from above, as Beethoven did. Above all, I realize at such moments the tremendous significance of Jesus' supreme revelation, "I and my Father are one." Those vibrations assume the forms of distinct mental images, after I have formulated my desire and resolve in regard to what I want—namely, to be inspired so that I can compose something that will uplift and benefit humanity—something of permanent value.
>
> Straightaway the ideas flow in upon me, directly from God, and not only do I see distinct themes in my mind's eye, but they are clothed in the right forms, harmonies and orchestration. Measure by measure, the finished product is revealed to me when I am in those rare, inspired moods.[12]

These personal disclosures of Brahms' metaphysical approach to composition make less surprising the revelations of Katharine Trevelyan about the nature of music, both cosmic and earthly. During a mystical interlude, Katharine was given the following insights. "I saw conceptions like the motet '*Furchte Dich Nicht*' which we had just been singing a month before, as having an eternal shape—as having always been there, and Bach but embodying it, bring it to earth. I found that music was the purest of links between people, far surpassing in clarity our words or deeds, which were always smudged by personality."[13] At another point during the experience, she realized that she was hearing the "music of the spheres," which she had believed until then was a poetical fancy. "Now I got the distinct impression that the sound was caused by the movement in the heavens, and also that all music composed on earth was the result of people hearing this heavenly music within themselves, even if not consciously."[14]

It is not surprising then that music thus inspired could serve as a stimulant for a mystical experience in others. The experience reported below was triggered by the singing of the *Te Deum* in a village church. It happened outside our earthly time frame, as the *Te Deum* was continuing when the experience ended. At first, aware of a bluish smoke that seemed to rise from the stone floors, the person experiencing it then realized he was seeing "a soft impalpable self-luminous haze of violet colour" that extended farther than the walls and the roof of the building. He was able to look through the walls and see the landscape beyond where, he said, "I saw all parts of my being simultaneously, not from my eyes only.... Yet for all this intensified perceptive power there was no loss of touch with my physical surroundings, no suspension of my faculties of sense.... I felt happiness and peace beyond words." His account continues:

> Upon that instant the luminous haze engulfing me and all around me became transformed into golden glory, into light untellable.... The golden light of which the violet haze seemed now to have been as the veil or outer fringe, welled forth from a central immense globe of brilliancy.... But the most wonderful thing was that these shafts and waves of light, that vast expanse of photo-sphere, and even the great central globe itself, were crowded to solidarity with the forms of

living creatures ... a single coherent organism filling all place and space, yet composed of an infinitude of individuated existences....

But this vast spectacle of heaven and earth was succeeded by an even richer experience; one in which everything in time and space and form vanished from my consciousness and only the ineffable eternal things remained.... And as the point of a candle-flame leaps suddenly upward, when an object is held just above it, so the flame of my consciousness leapt to its utmost limit and passed into the region of the formless and uncreated to tell of which all words fail.[15]

The mind has, among other purposes, a focusing function. We are always bombarded with more data—mental, emotional, and physical—than we can assimilate at any one time. The brain-mind, through conditioning and ego-centered interests, serves to reduce these stimuli to a level that does not overwhelm our capacity to handle them. However, our ego-centered interests also cause us to be blind to a reality that always pervades us, but that we do not see. When we ourselves are somewhat prepared—as plowed ground, you might say—we can be confronted with a stimulus and/or a mental state that momentarily distracts the "I, me, mine" consciousness and allows in the awareness of this other reality. The Persian mystic, Suhrawerdi, expressed an interesting idea about the onset of a mystical awakening. "It may be an external stimulus ... which opens the prepared mind to the flash. We may take this to signify, not that the enlightenment is *due* to the stimulus, but that, when the self is ripe for the experience, the particular moment of enlightenment may be determined by any factor which increases the intensity with which the whole man lives. The sudden flash is, in itself, of minor importance only; it is merely a signal showing that the point has been reached at which the fusion of reasoned thought and emotional consciousness comes to fulfilment."[16]

In the following experience, two triggers—the stunning beauty of nature and an intense inner questioning—combine to shift this person's consciousness into a different dimension.

Born in the mountains of Lebanon, I have always loved the solitude of high peaks and deep gorges, and found peace in the company of fantastic rock formations.... It was late summer afternoon, cool, clear and peaceful. I sat on a solitary rock, in the shade of a high wall of cliffs. Before me sloped to a deep gorge a stretch of land spattered with rocks and trees. Immediately to the left of me rose, almost perpendicularly, the rugged Mt. Saneen—one of the highest and loveliest peaks of the Lebanon range. Now and then I could hear the twittering of a bird, the bleating of a ewe, or the bellowing of a cow.

Drifting from one thing to another, my thoughts were finally caught in the net of such questions as to How? and When? and Why? and by Whom? all this came to be. Such questions had long been besieging me, although I was yet between 20 and 21 years of age. Oblivious of everything about me, I began to feel like one labouring in an endless labyrinth and seeking a way out. The search, however, did not seem to oppress me. On the contrary, I felt as if goaded on and on, and as if I were on the verge of breaking through.

Now subsiding, now flaring up, that feeling did not leave me until I suddenly emerged out of the labyrinth into a world flooded in dazzling light. How long I laboured in that labyrinth I do not recall. How long the sensation of light stayed with me—that also is hard to confine in seconds. It seemed like a fleeting twinkle of an eye; and it also seemed like an eternity.

So poignant, so deep, was that experience, that for the rest of the day, and for many days after, I lived and moved as one lifted on wings and given a glimpse of Paradise. Nothing about me seemed alien to me, or unworthy of my love. I was at peace with all things.[17]

Starr Daily, as we recall, was illumined while in solitary confinement. Arthur Koestler had a mystical experience while in a Spanish prison. Another enlightenment took place in a prison in Egypt. This particular experience is important not only as an example of the catalyst of confinement combined with an inner searching, but also because it made an impact on our whole modern world.

In cell 54 in an Egyptian prison, Anwar Sadat was profoundly changed. In his autobiography, *In Search of Identity*, Sadat wrote that "two places in this world make it impossible for a man to escape from himself: a battlefield and a prison cell." Anwar Sadat, however, did not seek to escape from himself. On the contrary, he used the "opportunity" of imprisonment for deep introspection and soul-searching. "Now in the complete solitude of Cell 54, when I had no links at all with the outside world ... the only way in which I could break my loneliness was, paradoxically, to seek the companionship of that inner entity I call 'self.' "[18]

Cell 54 was bare—no bed, table, or chair. Only a palm-fiber mat and a dirty blanket lay upon the dank floor which was surrounded by walls that oozed water and huge "armies of bugs." The prisoners were forced to use crowded, filthy toilets which caused much illness. For most of his time in prison, Sadat was allowed only fifteen minutes each day to walk outside the cell.

After many months he was allowed reading material and began to read voraciously. An article by an American psychologist in an issue of *Reader's Digest* proved to be another stimulant to the transformation of Sadat's consciousness. The article suggested that even though there are times in a man's life when he might feel that "all avenues in front of him are blocked, that life itself is a prison cell with a perpetually locked door ... there is more than one key to this door.... No problem should ever be regarded as insuperable." The philosophy of this article, Sadat revealed, "opened infinite horizons of love before me."[19] While in prison, Sadat also read writings of some of the mystics who, he said, "appealed to me tremendously as I found in them an expression of such inarticulate, almost unconscious feelings as I experienced at the time."

The following excerpts from *In Search of Identity* give insight into the mystical transformation of consciousness that Sadat underwent in cell 54.

> Once released from the narrow confines of the "self," with its mundane suffering and petty emotions, a man will have stepped into a new, undiscovered world which is vaster and richer. His soul would enjoy absolute freedom, uniting with existence in its entirety, transcending time and space. Through this process of liberation, the human will develops into a love-force, and all earthly forces ... come to contribute to the achievement of perfect inner peace, and so provide a man with absolute happiness....
> Now that I had discovered and actually begun to live in that "new world," things began

to change. My narrow self ceased to exist and the only recognizable entity was the totality of existence, which aspired to a higher, transcendental reality. It was genuinely a conquest, for in that world I came to experience friendship with God ....

My friendship with God changed me a great deal. Only in defense of a just cause would I take up arms, so to speak. For now I felt I had stepped into a vaster and more beautiful world and my capacity for endurance redoubled....

It was in Cell 54 that I discovered that love is truly the key to everything. When the heavy shackles that had bound me to my "narrow self" were removed, I began to enjoy God's love. I felt I lived in His love, that love was a law of life. In love, life—nay, being itself—becomes possible; without love, being comes to an end.

When my individual entity merged into the vaster entity of all existence, my point of departure became love of home (Egypt), love of all being, love of God.[20]

Sadat's experience is another example of a time when spiritual growth and joy transcended the outward appearance. Sadat wrote, "I regard my last eight months in prison as the happiest period in my life. It was then that I was initiated into that new world of self-abnegation which enabled my soul to merge into all other beings, to expand and establish communion with the Lord of all Being."

It was probably this experience that led Sadat, when he became president of Egypt in 1970, to put forth an Initiative for Peace (documented in his book *In Search of Identity*). Although Sadat was certainly an Egyptian patriot and wanted what was best for Egypt, it is also clear that the philosophy and insights he gained in cell 54 led, after the

October war, to his remarkable overture toward peace in the Middle East when he devised and then carried through an unprecedented visit to Israel to speak at the Knesset—the beginning of the serious efforts toward peace which ended in the Israeli/Egyptian Camp David Accords.

"When the student is ready, the teacher will appear" is a familiar metaphysical teaching. While this statement may be true, it does not always fit our expectations. The teacher can be a person, but can just as easily be a book, poem, or article picked up "by chance." The teacher can be the higher self goading a person on in certain directions, a great spiritual leader, a neighbor, or even a child. In the East, there is the tradition of the guru (teacher) and ashram, which includes a circle of disciples who look to the spiritually enlightened teacher for direction. In the West, there are similar relationships, but not usually so formalized.

There are times when a master knows that a student is ready for illumination and the catalyst needed is merely a physical touch. Such was the case with Paramahansa Yogananda and his guru Sri Yukteswar. Yogananda wrote of the transforming power of his master's touch: "At his touch a great light broke upon my being, like the glory of countless suns blazing together. A flood of ineffable bliss overwhelmed my heart to an innermost core."[21] At another time Yogananda received full illumination at his master's hand.

> My body became immovably rooted; breath was drawn out of my lungs as if by some huge magnet. Soul and mind instantly lost their physical bondage and streamed out like a fluid piercing light from my every pore. The flesh was as though dead; yet in my intense awareness I knew that never before had I been fully alive. My sense of identity was no longer

narrowly confined to a body but embraced the circumambient atoms. People on distant streets seemed to be moving gently over my own remote periphery. The roots of plants and trees appeared through a dim transparency of the soil; I discerned the inward flow of their sap.

The whole vicinity lay bare before me. My ordinary frontal vision was now changed to a vast spherical sight, simultaneously all-perceptive. Through the back of my head I saw men strolling far down Rai Ghat Lane, and noticed also a white cow that was leisurely approaching....

All objects within my panoramic gaze trembled and vibrated like quick motion pictures. My body, Master's, the pillared courtyard, the furniture and floor, the trees and sunshine, occasionally became violently agitated, until all melted into a luminescent sea; even as sugar crystals, thrown into a glass of water, dissolve after being shaken. The unifying light alternated with materializations of form, the metamorphoses revealing the law of cause and effect in creation.

An oceanic joy broke upon calm endless shores of my soul. The Spirit of God, I realized, is exhaustless Bliss; His body is countless tissues of light. A swelling glory within me began to envelop towns, continents, the earth, solar and stellar systems, tenuous nebulae, and floating universes. The entire cosmos, gently luminous, like a city seen afar at night, glimmered within the infinitude of my being. The dazzling light beyond the sharply etched global outlines faded slightly at the farthest edges; there I saw a mellow radiance, ever undiminished. It was indescribably subtle; the planetary pictures were formed of a grosser light.

The divine dispersion of rays poured from an Eternal Source, blazing into galaxies, transfigured with ineffable auras. Again and again I saw the creative beams condense into constellations, then resolve into sheets of transparent flame. By rhythmic reversion, sextillion worlds passed into diaphanous luster, then fire became firmament.

I cognized the center of the empyrean as a point of intuitive perception in my heart. Irradiating splendor issued from my nucleus to every part of the universal structure. Blissful *amrita*, nectar of immortality, pulsated through me with a quicksilverlike fluidity.[22]

When the breath returned suddenly to Yogananda's lungs, his disappointment was unbearable. He fell at his guru's feet in gratitude for this cosmic experience. His Master, however, said, "You must not get overdrunk with ecstasy. Much work yet remains for you in the world. Come, let us sweep the balcony floor; then we shall walk by the Ganges."[23]

As his guru had predicted, Yogananada was the first great master of India to be called to the West. His *Autobiography of a Yogi*, a classic, is a font of knowledge about the Eastern master-student relationships and the teachings of Yoga.

Usually, in either the East or West, one of the first instructions of the spiritual teacher to the student is to begin the practice of meditation. It is the purpose of the true master to help disciples find the divine within themselves. To find the "Christ in you, the hope of glory" (Col. 1:27), as Paul called it, the student is directed inward into his or her own consciousness, "by *letting go* and *sinking deeply into yourself* where awareness of the equality of all being will make itself known to you. *Then it will dawn on you that you are all angel and with all the angels,*" taught Meister Eckhart. "As we are emptied of ourselves, we take within us Christ, God, bliss and holiness."[24]

Joel Goldsmith teaches a similar wisdom:

> The purpose of a mystical teaching is to reveal the son of God within. It is not to instill in us the worship of another deity in the person of the founder of a new religion. True, every spiritual teacher must evoke gratitude and appreciation because of his life of dedication, but not worship. The real mission of the teacher and his teaching is to turn us back within ourselves until we, too, like the teacher, receive impartations. When this begins in our experience, the earth melts, the problems disappear; the discordant experiences of earth are resolved and dissolved—not by any wisdom that we have, not by what we have learned in books, but by the thunder of that silence which is within us."[25]

In the next chapter, we will examine the "thunder of silence" of which Goldsmith speaks, for meditation is perhaps the most effective catalyst for the mystical experience. We will also explore The Mystic Path which continues to summon the mystic seeker.

The Enterprise

Steps on the Mystic Path

T he human heart can go the lengths of God.
Dark and cold we may be, but this
Is no winter now. The frozen misery
Of centuries breaks, cracks, begins to move,
The thunder is the thunder of the floes,
The thaw, the flood, the upstart Spring.
Thank God our time is now when wrong
Comes up to face us everywhere,
Never to leave us till we take
The longest stride of soul men ever took.
Affairs are now soul size.
The enterprise
Is exploration into God.

   —*From* A Sleep of Prisoners *by Christopher Fry*

Prayer, or *speaking* our hearts to the divine Source, is often the beginning of a movement inward, but eventually meditation, or *listening* to the divine Source, must take over. "If prayer is to be effective," taught Goldsmith, "whatever words or thoughts we use in the preliminary stages of prayer must eventually come to a stop, and we must retire within in the attitude of 'Speak, Lord; for thy servant heareth.' Whether it takes a day, a year, or many years, it is imperative to have those periods of silence until we do hear that still small voice within and feel the Presence and Its power."[1]

Vanora Goodhart, an English artist, was introduced to meditation techniques by a book on Zen Buddhism written by Christmas Humphries, an English judge. Through meditation, she experienced deep inner peace and felt radiantly happy. Eventually, Vanora came under the influence of a spiritual teacher and healer, who encouraged her to continue with meditation. Late in 1977 she had the following experience while meditating:

> ... I felt a stirring at the base of my spine, and a slight pressure that rose up my back, at the same time a light began seeping through my closed eyelids, bright and gentle at first, but growing more and more intense. Frankly, I have a very analytical mind and I immediately tried to rationalise what was happening. Momentarily, I opened my eyes to make sure this Light was not coming from anywhere in the room—it was most certainly not.
>
> I closed my eyes again. The intensity grew and grew. If my eyes had been open I should have felt it was blinding. Moreover, there was a great power and strength in this Light, that was by now burning wonderfully deep into my emotions. The bliss was so totally overwhelming,

that the still rationalizing part of me wondered whether I could bear it—was I dying, was I leaving my body? The pins and needles that started in my head were now spreading down through my body, at the same time I felt I was being drawn upwards and in a great and wonderful rush of power that rose eventually to a crescendo and bathed me through and through with glorious burning, embracing Light. Then slowly, gently, I came back, again there was the powerful feeling of being drawn, this time back down into my body. During this time I had at one point flung my arms open as if I wanted to open my heart physically to the Light."[2]

Meditation, even over many years, does not guarantee the spiritual aspirant a mystical illumination. It is a preparation, however, that is necessary on the spiritual path and always brings closer that time when we, too, will be infused with divine understanding. "The grace from above," it is said, "requires preparation from below." Besides opening the door to the transcendent, meditation enhances our well-being in everyday life and brings an inner assurance and a peaceful mind.

The mystical way, the infinite way, is not the way of the sword; it is not the way of might or force: it is the way of stillness. Sooner or later we must see that within us there is an inner realm. It will answer every question. It will teach us in the only place where we can be taught—within. The still small voice will instruct us in whatever our particular gift, talent, or field may be, whether in spiritual or mathematical wisdom, art, literature, science, or music.[3]

Moreover, meditation is not only beneficial to our individual development; it is also a world service. "Every time that we meditate ...," wrote Goldsmith, "we are ... lessening the evil and selfish influences in the world. The degree to which evil seems to be lessened may be of minute proportions ... but once the Spirit is loosed, there are no limits to Its far-reaching effects because there is no such thing as a little of Spirit or a little power in this Spirit."[4]

> When the grace of God is received in your consciousness and mine, it is not a static and limited something embodied somewhere within our frame: it is a light that permeates us and flows out through us and from us; and inasmuch as there are no barriers to the activity of Spirit, this light which we have received as the result of our union with our Source flows out through the walls and windows of our homes into the world and becomes a leaven wherever an individual is raising his thought to God, regardless of what concept of God he may entertain. Whether he be in a hospital or in a prison, whether he be walking the earth free or be living in some nation where he is in slavery, if he is lifting his thought above human power, to whatever may be his concept of the Divine, the light which goes out from us and through us because of our meditation reaches that receptive Soul, and in some measure lightens his burden, sometimes freeing him from sin, disease, and false appetites.[5]

The practice of meditation often leads the serious spiritual seeker toward the Mystic Way or Path, and is also the instrument of continued progress along that path. The

Mystic Way, according to Evelyn Underhill, is no less than the process of "the transmuting of 'earthly' into 'heavenly' man." Although the traveler on this path may make many detours, turns, and stops when "earthly" man, or the separate ego, asserts its will, there are five definitive steps or stages of growth: the awakening of the self, purgation or purification, illumination, the "dark night of the soul," and, finally, union.

The Awakening

Circumstances of life again and again tend to lead us toward the same conclusions that Matthew Arnold expressed in "Dover Beach."

> ... the world, which seems
> To lie before us like a land of dreams,
> So various, so beautiful, so new,
> Hath really neither joy, nor love, nor light,
> Nor certitude, nor peace, nor help for pain;
> And we are here as on a darkling plain
> Swept with confused alarms of struggle and
>   flight,
> Where ignorant armies clash by night.

It finally dawns on our consciousness that there must be a better way to live; this world *as we experience it* does not live up to our expectations. We believe that there must be more to life, and we cry to "whatever God may be" to help us find it. We are now ready for an *awakening* to a new reality, to consciousness of a divine Reality. We probably are not ready to completely give up the "old self" because we are too entrenched in the patterns of material thought which have governed our lives and wrapped us in layers of conditioning. But a window has been opened. Although sometimes a mystical experience will dramatically set us on the path, a steady growth in consciousness and a determination to find Truth serves the same purpose.

Purgation and Purification

As our consciousness grows, we realize that we are participants in our destiny, that we are not innocent bystanders, or at least we need not be. At the same time, we grow more aware that, although our feet might rest on clay, our spirit can soar to the heavens. We become aware of those who have made passage; scriptures and spiritual writings come alive for us and have a meaning that had remained quiescent through previous readings.

There is a medieval allegory that describes the quest of the Philosopher's Stone as the hunting of the Green Lyon, which is symbolic of the potential of every creature to attain perfection.

> Our lyon wanting maturitie
> Is called greene for his unripeness, trust me:
> And yet full quickly he can run
> And soon can overtake the Sun.

And so it is, when we perceive a divine Reality, the pursuit of which is the only worthwhile quest, we begin looking within ourselves to remove the clouds that obscure this sun. This is a time of self-examination, self-discipline, and perfection of character by overcoming self-centeredness.

The reward is great. "It is by losing the egocentric life," says Huxley, "that we save the hitherto latent and undiscovered life which, in the spiritual part of our being, we share with the divine Ground. The new-found life is 'more abundant' than the other, and of a different and higher kind. Its possession is liberation into the eternal, and liberation is beatitude."[6]

Whether by choice or by circumstance, giving up our dependence on material possession can be fortuitous for our soul. Anwar Sadat testified to the spiritual benefits of the ascetic life.

> Inside Cell 54, as my material needs grew increasingly less, the ties which had bound me to the material world began to be severed, one after another. My soul, having jettisoned its earthly freight, was freed and so took off like a bird soaring into space, into the furthest regions of existence, into infinity. So long as a man is enslaved by material needs—wanting to be or to possess one thing or another—nothing will ever belong to him; he will always belong to "things."[7]

St. John of the Cross shared his wisdom about the process of purification in the following verse.

> That you may have pleasure in everything
> Seek your own pleasure in nothing....
> That you may possess all things
> Seek to possess nothing.
> That you may be everything
> Seek to be nothing.

Illumination

The intensity of the mystical experience, as we have seen from many examples, varies from the sudden flash of insight into the mysteries of reality and the renewed faith in a loving and benevolent universe it brings to complete revelation of the ultimate transcendent truth. Evelyn Underhill has described this stage of illumination as "the great swing back into sunshine which is the reward of that painful descent into the 'cell of self-knowledge'." This "swing back into the sunshine" is precipitated by a "lifting of consciousness from a self-centred to a God-centred world [and] is of the essence of illumination."[8] At this stage, the mystic has access to a higher level of consciousness than is available to an ordinary person. Although he or she does not partake of it continually, cosmic consciousness has become accessible. He or she often experiences blissful states and is conscious of the presence of God. The following poem by Rabindranath Tagore expresses the consciousness of the illuminated mystic:

> Yours is the light that breaks forth from the
>   dark, and the good that sprouts from the
>   cleft heart of strife.
> Yours is the house that opens upon the world,
>   and the love that calls to the battlefield.
> Yours is the gift that still is a gain when
>   everything is a loss, and the life that flows
>   through the caverns of death.
> Yours is the heaven that lies in the common
>   dust, and you are there for me, you are
>   there for all.

The Dark Night of the Soul

It seems as if the spiritual journey should end happily in the stage of illumination, and many people do choose to stop there, or are temporarily deceived that it is the final destination, yet the mystic path continues. Even though the person who has achieved this special consciousness is aware of God's presence and even of the unity of all life, continuous conscious union remains to be achieved. This union requires the final letting-go of the individual ego. "Those who go on," Underhill has said, "are the great and strong spirits, who do not seek to *know*, but are driven to *be*."[9]

The Dark Night of the Soul that these "strong spirits" encounter is the name for the painful and negative state that usually intervenes between the Illuminative and the Unitive Life. It is now that the spiritual seeker meets the most challenging paradox: you must lose your life to find it. The aspirant experiences the Dark Night in that time when he or she, through faith, is learning to give up everything and become a purified vehicle for the expression of God. Left with nothing, not even the spiritual joys of closeness to God so dearly won, the soul feels abandoned and often despairs. "But before real and permanent union with the Absolute can take place," wrote Underhill, "before the whole self can learn to live on those high levels where—its being utterly surrendered to the Infinite Will—it can be wholly transmuted in God, merged in the great life of the All, this dependence on personal joys must be done away."[10] It is the final period of testing, and those who make it through have won a great battle.

Many people have experienced, even at earlier levels of spiritual attainment, versions of the Dark Night of the Soul. Raynor Johnson has described this well in *Watcher on the Hills*. "They may have had glimpses of near-Illuminative levels, but after the rapture a reaction sets in, and they surge back into self-dissatisfaction, despair, frustration and the darkest of nights.... They had a glimpse of the Delectable Mountains, and assumed that they had almost arrived." Johnson feels this happens because the soul's growth has been too rapid. "Spiritual distances," he says,

"can be deceptive, and disappointment can be correspond-
ingly great."[11]

The Unitive Life

"The self which comes forth from the night is no
separated self ... but the New Man, the transmuted
humanity, whose life is *one* with the Absolute Life of God."[12]
The goal is attained; the sun shines now, not on us but
through us. Again, we shall go to Evelyn Underhill, the great
master of mystical knowledge, for the characteristics of the
Unitive Life:

> (1) a complete absorption in the interests of
> the Infinite, under whatever mode It is appre-
> hended by the self; (2) a consciousness of
> sharing Its strength, acting by Its authority,
> which results in a complete sense of freedom,
> an invulnerable serenity, and usually urges the
> self to some form of heroic effort or creative
> activity; (3) the establishment of the self as a
> "power for life," a centre of energy, an actual
> parent of spiritual vitality in other men.

There are those people who have attained the Unitive
Life whose names are not written in history. Many we do
know, however, particularly the great religious mystics who
have shared their journey in writings and journals.

Meister Eckhart expressed the qualities of the unitive life
as he called others toward it: "Each of us should be a
heaven in which God dwells." Richard of St. Victor describes
the attainment of the unitive state with this penetrating
analogy: "When the soul is plunged in the fire of divine
love, like iron, it first loses its blackness, and then growing
to white heat, it becomes like unto the fire itself. And lastly,

it grows liquid, and losing its nature is transmuted into an utterly different quality of being."[13]

Once found, one recognizes this new life as the natural life. The prodigal son has returned. Referring to Ruysbroeck of the fourteenth century, whom Underhill called one of the greatest mystics the world has ever known, Underhill explains, "The mystic in the unitive state is living in and of his native land; no exploring alien, but a returned exile, now wholly identified with it, part of it, yet retaining his personality intact."[14]

Blessed Henry Suso, also a visionary and mystic of the fourteenth century, expressed in the *Book of Truth* the joyful intoxication of complete immersion of the self in God in the following passage:

> When the good and faithful servant enters
> into the joy of his Lord, he is inebriated by the
> riches of the house of God; for he feels, in an
> ineffable degree, that which is felt by an
> inebriated man. He forgets himself, he is no
> longer conscious of his selfhood; he disappears
> and loses himself in God, and becomes one
> spirit with Him, as a drop of water which is
> drowned in a great quantity of wine.[15]

Jalalu 'd Din, the Persian mystic, also uses the image of wine as he expresses the joy of the unitive life in his poem "The Festival of Spring."

> With Thy Sweet Soul, this soul of mine
> Hath mixed as Water doth with Wine.
> Who can the Wine and Water part,
> Or me and Thee when we combine?
> Thou art become my greater self;
> Small bounds no more can me confine.
> Thou hast my being taken on,

And shall not I now take on Thine?
Me Thou for ever has affirmed,
That I may ever know Thee mine.
Thy Love has pierced me through and through,
Its thrill with Bone and Nerve entwine.
I rest as Flute laid on Thy lips;
A lute, I on Thy breast recline.
Breathe deep in me that I may sigh;
Yet strike my strings, and tears shall shine.

We need not look only to the far past for evidence of the mystic who has achieved the unitive life. In 1955 Teilhard de Chardin, during the last months of his life, wrote to a friend: "I now live permanently in the presence of God."[16]

Jae Jah Noh, the founder of The Aspen Grove, a spiritual community located in Denver, Colorado, testifies in his book *Do You See What I See?*, to his development from his first mystical experience to a stage of living within the divine Presence.

I soon realized that a basic alteration in my mind, my intelligence, my mode of thinking and my access to wisdom, had occurred, and was continuing. The experience was not a singular event, but a living, on-going process, which I was currently participating in. Here was the gift of a new "tool", and I was only slowly beginning to realize and utilize its potential.

This experience has slowly matured into a living reality, an ongoing experience of the transcendental. I am never without it. I am never outside this living presence.[17]

Bernadette Roberts, in her book *The Experience of No-Self*, describes her experience of the end of the "homeward journey."

The disintegration of personal selfhood is just the beginning of this dissolution—this homeward journey—and there is no point along the route at which anyone could say "now I am God"—it would make no sense. At the same time, there is no point at which we are not part of God, and it is *this* point which is clearly seen once the "I am" has dissolved. That which remains is discovered to be that which was there before the "I am" ever arose.[18]

Lest we conclude, however, that these mystics, once their "immense journey" is achieved, are content to retire from the world to enjoy the inner fruits of their accomplishments, we need only look further to find the outer fruits. Although retirement from the world might sometimes be necessary for the development of the mystical consciousness, the majority of the mystically illumined return to the world energized by a spiritual energy.

The great historian Arnold Toynbee in *Study of History* wrote about the process of withdrawal and return characteristic of many of those following the Mystic Way.

Creative personalities when they are taking the mystic path which is their highest spiritual level ... belong to the duality of movement we call ... withdrawal and return. The withdrawal makes possible for the personality to realize powers within itself which might have remained dormant if he had not been released for the time being from his social toils and turmoils ... but a transfiguration in solitude can have no purpose, and perhaps even no meaning, except as a prelude to the return of the transfigured personality into the social milieu out of which he originally came.... The return is the essence of the whole movement as well as its final cause.[19]

A study of mystical literature shows, almost to astonishment, how many of the great works of humankind have been accomplished, or at least begun, by the mystically illumined throughout history. These accomplishments are not only in such areas as religion, art, and literature, but in the "practical" affairs of the world as well. "The great unitive mystics," wrote Evelyn Underhill, "are each of them the founders of spiritual families, centres wherefrom radiates new transcendental life. The 'flowing light of the Godhead' is focussed in them, as in a lens, only that it may pass through them to spread out on every side."[20] Examples can barely suggest the quantity, depth, and diversity of their work.

St. Teresa of Avila, after breaking through her long seige of the Purgative Way into the Unitive Life, was moved by an inward voice to start a new life reforming the great Carmelite Religious Order. St. Catherine of Siena, after a three-year retreat, returned to active life as a dominant force in the politics of Italy. "The soul enamoured of My Truth," spoke God to St. Catherine, "never ceases to serve the whole world in general."[21]

St. Ignatius Loyola founded the Jesuit Order, which became a potent force in Europe and is today known as an irrepressible force for social justice as well as a bastion of excellence in education. William James said of St. Ignatius that "his mysticism made him assuredly one of the most powerfully practical human engines that ever lived."[22]

Another Jesuit, Teilhard de Chardin, referred to many times in these pages, was a renowned anthropologist who contributed much to his field besides writing religious and philosophical works that have led a movement toward the reconciliation of religion and science. His work advanced the mystical consciousness of many of his "disciples in thought."

The remarkable work of Myrtle and Charles Fillmore has had a profound influence on modern religious thought and practice. Against great odds, they founded the Unity School of Christianity, which itself is explicit of mystical teaching, concentrating on the commonalities of the different religions rather than their differences. Said Charles Fillmore, "We see the good in all religions and we want everyone to feel free to find the Truth for himself wherever he may be led to find it."[23]

We have already noted the contribution toward peace made by Anwar Sadat in recent history. Another mystic, Dag Hammarskjöld, the second Secretary General of the United Nations, was known for his passion and his tireless and dedicated work for peace and justice throughout the world. His journal, *Markings*, documents his spiritual journey into mystical consciousness, the inner life that allowed him to be effective where other less selfless people were not. "He [Hammarskjöld] had no need for the divided responsibility in which others seek to be safe from ridicule, because he had been granted a faith which required no confirmation—a contact with reality, light and intense like the touch of a loved hand: a union in self-surrender without self-destruction, where his heart was lucid and his mind loving."[24]

The gifts of music, art, and literature to the world by mystics are beyond documentation here. The few examples mentioned throughout this book serve only to suggest the depth and breadth of their contribution toward the sustenance and cultivation of beauty, sanity, and spiritual values in the world. Artists who are genuine mystics are truly "Ambassadors of God."

Although there are contemplatives whose invaluable contribution to humanity is primarily through prayer and devotion, The Mystic Way most often leads back to the world. Yet it is a world renewed, in the eyes of mystics, by the light of a Transcendent Reality that illumines and makes straight their path. The words of J. C. Gowan urge us to begin the pilgrimage. "There is an El Dorado; the map is outlined, the way is through the inner reaches of the latent powers of man's mind, and, knowing that it exists, having the map and the road, it behooves us all to start on the immense journey."

Where Shall I Find Thee?

The World
Transformed

L ord, where shall I find Thee?
High and hidden in Thy place;
And where shall I not find Thee?
The world is full of Thy glory.
I have sought Thy nearness;
With all my heart have I called Thee.
And going out to meet Thee
I found Thee coming toward me.
                              —Judah Halevi

Let there be many windows in your soul,
That all the glory of the universe
May beautify it. Not the narrow pane
Of one poor creed can catch the radiant rays
That shine from countless sources. Tear away
The blinds of superstition: let the light
Pour through fair windows, broad as truth itself
And high as heaven.
                              —Ralph Waldo Trine

"Take courage, for the human race is divine," wrote Pythagoras, the great Greek philosopher of the sixth century B.C.

We might be discouraged by the date of this statement and wonder why, if what he says is true, we have lagged so far behind in this realization, why we still have wars, and cruelty, and injustice in the world. The answer may be that our collective human journey toward self-realization is made individually, one by one by one. "Prodigals of perversity," we journey home alone, leaning only, as Edgar Cayce suggested, on the arm of someone we have helped.

The grace of the mystical encounter, experienced or even read about, gives us a foretaste (or perhaps more accurately a remembrance) of this divine life which is our birthright as sons and daughters of a divine Creator. The significance of the "holy instant" for those individuals who experience it is undeniable. The portent for the future of us all is momentous. In *Human Destiny*, Lecomte du Noüy argues that evolution is not over for humankind. Mystics, he believed, are transitional forms, forerunners of our divine potential.

The prominent psychologist Abraham Maslow, disturbed by the trend of psychology to define humankind by its pathology, undertook a study of mentally and emotionally healthy people. After identifying this group, whom he called self-actualized, and the qualities and values that they exhibit (B- or being Values are described by Maslow in *Toward a Psychology of Being*), Maslow also discovered that these people tended to have a high incidence of what he termed peak-experiences (secularized religious, mystical, or transcendental experiences). Maslow claims that "peakers" find these experiences self-validating, that in fact they are "*so* valuable that they make life worth while by their occasional occurrence."[1] This is what Sisirkumar Ghose, who wrote *Mystics as a Force for Change*, believes. He wrote: "There is, in fact, no other aim or theory of life that gives human life such dignity as the mystical.... Perhaps the greatest value of the ... doctrine is that it brings back meaning to life, the meaning of the Whole."[2] Rufus Jones, the great Quaker mystic (though it is almost redundant to say Quaker mystic), expressed the same thought. "In these highest mystical moments of contact with the real presence of God, there is a sense of having arrived at the goal of life."[3]

Maslow also found from his extensive study that "the world seen in the peak-experiences is seen only as beautiful, good, desirable, worthwhile, etc. and is never experienced as evil or undesirable."[4] It is reacted to with awe, wonder, amazement, humility, and even reverence, exaltation, and piety. An examination of mystical literature reveals exactly what Maslow found in his psychological studies. The following testimony, cited by a university professor who had a prolonged and intense mystical experience, attests to the significance it had for his life.

> I have been privileged to experience briefly and incompletely an aspect of the deeper reality. Like a traveller who has spent but an hour in a strange land, I could describe very little of it. Yet I know, absolutely and finally, that reality exists behind the material universe we perceive with our senses; that man potentially has the power to perceive this reality; that in this reality is a Source of love and goodness which man potentially is able to contact and draw from; and that the extent to which a person realises this potentiality is the most important fact about his life.[5]

J. Trevor, whom we have quoted earlier, also gives testimony to the impact of mystical illuminations on his life.

I have severely questioned the worth of these moments.... But I find that, after every questioning and test, they stand out to-day as the most real experiences of my life, and experiences which have explained and justified and unified all past experiences and all past growth. Indeed, their reality and their far-reaching significance are ever becoming more clear and evident. When they came, I was living the fullest, strongest, sanest, deepest life. I was not seeking them. What I was seeking, with resolute determination, was to live more intensely my own life, as against what I knew would be the adverse judgment of the world. It was in the most real seasons that the Real Presence came, and I was aware that I was immersed in the infinite ocean of God.[6]

However, the fact of the mystical experience and all that it signifies for the meaning of life has import beyond the individual alone. There are great implications in the mystic revelations for society and for the values that society should seek to express in its individual and corporate lives. Evolution has brought humankind to the brink of a precipice that looks downward to an abyss and upward to the heavens. We shall make the choice by action or default. The "abyss" contains garbage from the Western world and the tragedy of famine from the East and South. The "heavens" contain a new world where all humankind claims the solidarity and fellowship of dignity, respect, and love. The revelations of the mystics point us upward.

Sri Aurobindo, a mystic and one of the most profound thinkers of the modern world, founder of the revered spiritual community in Pondicherry, India, gives, in the following passage, an inciteful assessment of the social and moral predicament in which we find ourselves.

At present mankind is undergoing an
evolutionary crisis in which is concealed a
choice of its destiny, for a stage has been
reached in which the human mind has achieved
in certain directions an enormous development
while in others it stands arrested and bewil-
dered and can no longer find its way.... Man
has created a system of civilisation which has
become too big for his limited mental capacity
and understanding and his still more limited
spiritual and moral capacity to utilise and
manage, a too dangerous servant of his
blundering ego and its appetites.[7]

But Aurobindo does not leave us hanging over the abyss.
He finds hope, and the hope is from the wisdom of the
mystics—"A life of unity, mutuality and harmony born of a
deeper and wider truth of our being."[8]

It is fascinating how providence produces great spiritual
leaders at the same time in different areas of the world.
Teilhard de Chardin, whose life span paralleled that of Sri
Aurobindo, in many ways also paralleled his thinking. In
How I Believe, Teilhard wrote the following words:

The time is close at hand when mankind will
see that, precisely in virtue of its position in a
cosmic evolution which it has become capable
of discovering and criticizing, it now stands
biologically between the alternatives of suicide
and worship.[9]

And in *The Divine Milieu*, Teilhard wrote:

Humanity was sleeping—it is still sleeping—
imprisoned in the narrow joys of its little
closed loves. A tremendous spiritual power is
slumbering in the depths of our multitude,
which will manifest itself only when we have

learnt to *break down the barriers* of our egoisms and, by a fundamental recasting of our outlook, raise ourselves up to the habitual and practical vision of universal realities.[10]

In order for us to recognize the larger vision of the world of which the mystics speak, we must put aside the blinders that restrict our vision, the blinders of parochial interests and narrow dogmas. The most predominant revelation of the mystical experience is that we all are one, individual manifestations of a single spirit. Goldsmith poses the question of the ultimate meaning of that reality. "In the materialistic way of life," he wrote, "it is a natural thing, humanly, for us to be proud of being American, Canadian, English, German, or whatever our nationality may be. But what happens to that swashbuckling materialism when we discover our Self, when we discover that we all are brothers and sisters, regardless of the flag that flies over us, the color of our skin, or the church to which we belong."[11]

A Protestant and simple man of the seventeenth century, Hemme Hayen had a mystical illumination that lasted over several days. Among other things, he was shown "a little piece of the new earth." As do so many other mystics, Hayen said that he now understood spiritual teachings for the first time. At one point, after reading Isaiah, chapters 55 through 61, he claimed: "Then I understood everything according to the inner ground and saw very clearly how the Spirit of God speaks .... Indeed, whatever I read immediately became clear and shining in my heart ...." One thing which became very clear to Hayen was "how a person can come to God and that it does not depend on the sect, but only on seeking God with one's whole heart."[12]

Margaret Isherwood, while speaking of the religions of humankind, argues for a more ecumenical view.

They are many [religions], they are imperfect, but they too are not "islands" complete in themselves. Below the surface, in intention and direction, they are one, their deep common purposes being the unitive knowledge of God. And if it is true that "God hath not at any time left Himself without a witness", then it cannot also be true that He revealed himself to one people at one time only, and gave one formula for salvation to one Church alone....

An ancient Vedic hymn says with deep wisdom: "As different streams having their sources in different places mingle their waters in the sea, so, O lord, the different paths men take through different tendencies, various though they appear, crooked or straight, all lead to Thee."[13]

Arnold Toynbee professed similar ideas in *Christianity Among the Religions of the World*:

If God loves mankind, He would have made a revelation to us among other people.... It would also seem unlikely that He would not have made other revelations to other people as well. And it would seem unlikely that He would not have given His revelation in different forms, with different facets, and to different degrees, according to the difference in the nature of individual souls and in the nature of the local tradition of civilization. I should say that this view is a corollary of the Christian view of God as being love.[14]

It is certainly understandable that religions in their

expressions, traditions, and rituals are very different. They have developed at different times, among differing peoples and cultures, and within the languages of these cultures. Whether language is responsible for the development of difference in cultures, or differences in cultures are responsible for language is still being determined by semanticists. However, there is the certainty that they play upon each other, and there is much evidence that language can actually determine thought patterns. Therefore, since truths revealed in various religions were interpreted within a living language and culture—different from others—it is natural that they would take on some unique characteristics and meanings. Better understanding and social harmony can be achieved as we grow more aware of the influence of language and culture and recognize the unity underlying various revelations.

Although herself a Protestant, Evelyn Underhill, through her comprehensive study of mysticism, has come to the following conclusion. "Attempts ... to limit mystical truth—the direct apprehension of the Divine Substance—by the formulae of any one religion, are as futile as the attempt to identify a precious metal with the die which converts it into current coin.... But the gold from which this diverse coinage is struck is always the same precious metal: always the same Beatific Vision of a Goodness, Truth, and Beauty which is *one*."[15]

An appreciation of "unity in diversity" concerning religion, as well as other areas of culture, is usually the attitude of the mystic and of enlightened humanity in general. The urge not to change others, but to understand them, is the hallmark of the person who desires harmony and constructive cooperation.

> There are many paths that lead to the summit of one and the same mountains; their differences will be more apparent the lower

down we are, but they vanish at the peak; each will naturally take the one that starts from the point at which he finds himself; he who goes round about the mountain looking for another is not climbing. Never let us approach another believer to ask him to become "one of us", but approach him with respect as one who is already one of His.[16]

When we take this ecumenical approach, we allow ourselves to grow in spiritual understanding beyond the narrow limits of the dogmas into which we were born, for the teachings of the great religions are not mutually exclusive. "The missions of the higher religions," wrote Toynbee, "are not competitive; they are complementary. We can believe in our own religion without having to feel that it is the sole repository of truth. We can love it without having to feel that is the sole means of salvation."[17]

The revelations of the mystics have provided a core of revealed experience, of spiritual truths, that informs all major religions. As Maslow has written:

> The very beginning, the intrinsic core, the essence, the universal nucleus of every known high religion ... has been the private, lonely, personal illumination, revelation, or ecstasy of some acutely sensitive prophet or seer. The high religions call themselves revealed religions and each of them tends to rest its validity, its function, and its right to exist on the codification and the communication of this original mystic experience or revelation from the lonely prophet to the mass of human beings in general.[18]

Maslow feels that this core religious experience could be

the "meeting ground not only ... for Christians and Jews and Mohammedans," but for all peoples of diverse backgrounds.

Throughout their writings, religious leaders who are mystics are united in seeking tolerance and understanding between faiths. Abraham Isaac Kook, the late Chief Rabbi of Israel, was eloquent in his calling for a universal outlook between peoples.

> A person must liberate himself from confinement within his private concerns. This pervades his whole being so that all his thoughts focus only on his own destiny. It reduces him to the worst kind of smallness, and brings upon him endless physical and spiritual distress. It is necessary to raise a person's thought and will and his basic preoccupations toward universality, to the inclusion of all, to the whole world, to man, to the Jewish people, to all existence....
>
> The firmer a person's vision of universality, the greater the joy he will experience, and the more he will merit the grace of divine illumination. The reality of God's providence is discernible when the world is seen in its totality.[19]

Rabbi Kook saw a division of people into three types: one "who sings the song of his people," one "whose spirit extends beyond the boundary of Israel, to sing the song of man," and "one who rises even higher, uniting himself with the whole existence, with all creatures, with all worlds. With all of them he sings his song."[20]

Teilhard de Chardin also wrote eloquently of the movement of humankind toward greater unification in all aspects of life, including religion. "Teilhard compared the different religions with 'living branches' which are developing on a central stem. He also likened them to 'rivers' joining a stream or 'currents' within the one great river of mankind. At present, these 'currents' are still at cross-purposes but they can be seen as 'coming to run together.' "[21]

The reputation of Harry Emerson Fosdick far exceeded his role as minister of the Riverside Church in New York City. His writings were well known throughout the world, and he was a leader in Christian thinking. He, too, was a mystic, and the following passage gives an example of the universality of his thinking.

> All systems of theology are as transient as the cultures they are patterned from....
> All these theological systems and all others that will follow them are partial, tentative, contemporary formulations of great matters. To take the best insights in them all, to see the incompleteness and falsity in them all, to trust none of them as a *whole*, to see always that the Thing to be explained is infinitely greater than our tentative conditioned explanation—this seems to me wisdom....
> I have had experiences myself and have seen them in others that, inexplicable by any system of materialism, only the basic affirmations of religion, so it seems to me, can account for.[22]

Why, we might ask, with such enlightened religious leadership, are we still so far from the ideal of "unity in diversity," and the cooperation it would bring between diverse religions and nations: a cooperation that could make our planet bloom as we put away our weapons and use those resources to solve our social and economic needs, both local and global? First, it cannot be denied that in

Rabbi Kook's classification, many men and women, many religious and political leaders, still belong to type one: those who sing the song of their own people. Second, in the name of progress, mankind has created a new religion—science—and we make obeisance to its child—materialism. Science is, of course, extremely important, and its fruits should not be denied. However, by placing it first in our value system, above moral and spiritual values, it becomes a mindless machine with a purpose independent of people; it disregards means and ends and spews forth technology that can ultimately destroy those it was thought to serve. Andrew Greeley was particularly concerned with this issue when he wrote the following:

> The great heresy of the contemporary Western world is that the only kind of knowledge that is to be taken seriously and trusted is discursive, cognitive knowledge, that which is acquired by man's practical or technical reason. Concomitant with this are the assertions that the only kind of truth is that which can be empirically verified, and the only kind of language fit for human communication that of logically validated prose. In other words, that knowledge and language which is appropriate for discourse in the empirical sciences is the only one that is really worth developing in man, because it is the only one that can have any demonstrable validity.[23]

But there is another kind of knowledge—wisdom—and its roots are in mysticism. It says, "Have hope, do not despair." John Hill, mystic, philosopher and author of *The Enlightened Society*, believes that:

Correctly speaking, modern man is not sick in any traditional sense of the word. Instead, his malady is developmental rather than regressive; it is more akin to a "growing pain" than to a degenerative ailment....

Essentially, modern man suffers from being "between stages," psycho-spiritually speaking....

It is essential that the concept of *progress* take a new form....

In place of technological or financial progress, modern man must begin to orient his life around a psycho-spiritual vision of progress. Life should be lived not just to accumulate money, but to accumulate wisdom, not to develop a stock portfolio, but to develop oneself. Love and humor, not despair and cynicism, should mark his life.[24]

And, indeed, in spite of all the problems we see around us, there are places to look where hope and faith are justified and love is working its inevitable course. For progress toward the realization of human unity and oneness, we can celebrate the survival and growth of the United Nations. It is an embryonic organization reflecting the ultimate unity of humankind just as we humans are embryos of a higher self. It is an organization comprised of disparate nations, many of which have long been mortal enemies, yet the United Nations has yet provided those nations with a common ground. High officials in the United Nations testify that many disputes that could have led to worldwide conflict were defused in the halls and corridors of the UN. The United Nations is a physical manifestation of a spiritual reality, and though not yet perfected, it reflects the spiritual state that is being perfected in humankind, and so the two evolve together.

Behind the sensational headlines telling of the often bitter disagreement of nations as they debate in the General Assembly, the United Nations agencies quietly do their remarkable work for the whole community—animal, vegetable, and mineral—for the total good of Mother Earth. Agencies that address the problems of the environment, health, world resources, poverty, homelessness, and agriculture; those collecting necessary data, working toward global solutions, and giving much-needed aid work with little recognition and relatively small resources, building a network of world community.

There is also much hope in the movements for peace that are growing apace around the world and in the growing corps of people involved in citizen diplomacy through their individual recognition of the spiritual oneness that we share. There are many individuals and groups working for the environment and for the protection of animals. Finally, the Green Movement is gaining ground in the United States as well as in Europe, where it was begun. It advocates a holistic approach to problem solving and emphasizes that the state of the environment, the state of social justice, and the hope of peace require an astute assessment of means and ends in a moral and spiritual context. "Greens" believe with Teilhard that "The age of nations has passed. Now, unless we wish to perish we must shake off our old prejudices and build the earth."

There are also many resources now for those who wish to expand their consciousness and grow spiritually. That in itself is a sign that we are making progress, for, as was pointed out earlier, when the student is ready the master appears. One of the spiritual teachings that is available today gives us courage.

The way is not hard, but it *is* very different. Yours is the way of pain, of which God knows nothing. That way is hard indeed, and very lonely. Fear and grief are your guests, and they go with you and abide with you on the way. But the dark journey is not the way of God's Son. Walk in light and do not see the dark companions .... The Great Light always surrounds you and shines out from you.[25]

The same source suggests that we only need awaken; we have already reached our goal. "The journey to God is merely the reawakening of the knowledge of where you are always, and what you are forever. It is a journey without distance to a goal that has never changed."

The Quaker mystic Rufus Jones gives us good direction.

We have conquered the outward world, and put it in our nets, but the explorers of it are not yet "at home" in the universe. We have immensely improved the means of life, but we have somehow failed to discover to expand the *meaning and significance of life*.... We must explore the "labyrinthine ways" of our own selves. We must knock at the doors which lie within.... We have had our "Westward Ho", our "Northward Ho", our "Southward Ho",... but we now need a ringing call to "Inward Ho".[26]

When, one by one by one, we collectively reach a critical mass in spiritual consciousness, we can make a quantum leap into a new tomorrow. This has always been the call of the mystics.

CHAPTER 1

1. Julian of Norwich, *Showings*, Edmund
   Colledge, O.S.A. and James Walsh, S.J.
   (trans.), Paulist Press, New York, 1978,
   p. 52.

2. Starr Daily, *You Can Find God*, Fleming H.
   Revell Company, Westwood, N.J., 1963,
   p. 15.

3. Ibid., p. 17.

4. Nona Coxhead, *The Relevance of Bliss*, St.
   Martin's Press, New York, p. 44.

5. Arthur Koestler, *The Invisible Writing*, Stein
   and Day, New York, 1984, p. 427.

6. Ibid., pp. 429-430.

7. Paul Mendes-Flohr (ed.), *Ecstatic Confessions*,
   collected and introduced by Martin
   Buber, Harper & Row, San Francisco,
   1985, pp. 81-84.

8. Richard Maurice Bucke, M.D., *Cosmic
   Consciousness*, E. P. Dutton, New York,
   1901, p. 180.

9. Ibid., p. 180.

10. Ibid., p. 181.

11. Anne Fremantle (ed.), *The Protestant Mystics*,
    Little, Brown & Co., Boston, 1964, p. 45.

12. William James, *The Varieties of Religious
    Experience*, Modern Library, New York,
    1936, p. 402.

13. Bucke, p. 181.

CHAPTER 2

1. Evelyn Underhill, *Mysticism*, New American Library, New York, 1974, p. 447.

2. Richard Maurice Bucke, M.D., *Cosmic Consciousness*, E. P. Dutton, New York, 1901, p. 77.

3. Ibid., p. 3.

4. Ibid., pp. 9-10.

5. F. C. Happold, *Mysticism*, Penguin Books, Middlesex, England, 1970, p. 34.

6. Ibid., pp. 133-134.

7. Ibid., pp. 134-135.

8. Ibid., p. 135.

9. Pierre Teilhard de Chardin, *The Phenomenon of Man*, Harper & Row, New York, 1965, p. 36.

10. Ibid., p. 234.

11. Pierre Teilhard de Chardin, *The Divine Milieu*, Harper & Row, New York, 1960, p. 46, note.

12. Underhill, p. 445.

CHAPTER 3

1. Nona Coxhead, *The Relevance of Bliss*, St. Martin's Press, New York, 1985, p. 30.

2. Ibid., p. 31.

3. John Masefield, *So Long to Learn*, Macmillan, New York, 1952, p. 9.

4. Ibid., p. 9.

5. Ibid., p. 9.

6. Thomas E. Witherspoon, *Myrtle Fillmore: Mother of Unity*, Unity Books, Unity Village, Mo., 1977, p. 2.

7. *The Journal of Henry David Thoreau*, Houghton Mifflin, Boston, 1906, quoted by Anne Fremantle (ed.), *The Protestant Mystics*, Little, Brown & Co., Boston, 1964, pp. 243-244.

8. Margaret Isherwood, *The Root of the Matter*, Harper & Brothers, New York, 1954, p. 98.

9. J. Trevor, *My Quest for God*, London, 1897, pp. 268-269, quoted by William James, *The Varieties of Religious Experience*, Modern Library, New York, 1936, p. 388.

10. Evelyn Underhill, *Mysticism*, New American Library, New York, 1974, p. 422.

11. Irina Starr, *The Sound of Light*, De Vorss & Co., Marina Del Ray, Calif., 1974, pp. 1-2.

12. Claire Myers Owens, *Small Ecstasies*, A C S Publications, San Diego, Calif., 1983, p. 101.

13. William E. Kaufman, *Journeys: An Introductory Guide to Jewish Mysticism*, Bloch Publishing Company, New York, 1980, p. 37.

14. Underhill, p. 185.

15. Ibid., pp. 185-186.

CHAPTER 4

1. Emanuel Swedenborg, *Divine Love and Wisdom*, Citadel Press, New York, 1965, p. XX.

2. Ursula King, *Towards a New Mysticism: Teilhard de Chardin and Eastern Religions*, Seabury Press, New York, 1980, p. 205.

3. Sir Francis Younghusband, *Heart of Nature*, John Murray, Ltd., London, quoted by Raynor C. Johnson, *Watcher on the Hills*, Hodder and Stoughton, London, 1959, p. 85.

4. Raynor C. Johnson, *Watcher on the Hills*, Hodder and Stoughton, London, 1959, p. 23.

5. Ibid., pp. 84-85.

6. Nona Coxhead, *The Relevance of Bliss*, St. Martin's Press, New York, 1985, p. 43.

7. Johnson, p. 49.

8. King, p. 109.

9. Johnson, pp. 65-66.

10. Brother Mandus, *This Wondrous Way of Life*, quoted by Johnson, pp. 52-53.

11. Bernadette Roberts, *The Experience of No-Self*, Shambhala, Boston, 1985, p. 34.

12. Ibid., p. 30.

13. William E. Kaufman, *Journeys: An Introductory Guide to Jewish Mysticism*, Bloch Publishing Co., New York, 1980, p. 143.

14. J. Allen Boone, *Kinship With All Life*, Harper & Row, New York, 1954, p. 26.

15. *Breakthrough: Meister Eckhart's Creation Spirituality in New Translation*, introduction and commentaries by Matthew Fox, O.P., Doubleday, Garden City, N.Y., 1980, p. 98.

16. Ibid., p. 98.

CHAPTER 5

1. F. C. Happold, *Mysticism*, Penguin Books, Middlesex, England, 1970, p. 17.

2. Ken Wilber (ed.), *Quantum Questions: Mystical Writings of the World's Great Physicists*, Shambhala, Boulder, Colo., 1984, p. 7.

3. Arthur Eddington, *Science and the Unseen World*, George Allen & Unwin Ltd., London, 1929, pp. 21-22.

4. Ibid., pp. 23-24.

5. Erwin Schroedinger, "Why Not Talk Physics," Wilber, p. 81.

6. Erwin Schroedinger, "Oneness of Mind," Wilber, p. 89.

7. William James, *The Varieties of Religious Experience*, Modern Library, New York, 1936, p. 415.

8. Ibid, pp. 378-379.

9. Alfred Tennyson, in a letter to Mr. B. P. Blood, quoted by James, pp. 374-375.

10. W. T. Stace, *Mysticism and Philosophy*, Jeremy P. Tarcher, Inc., New York, 1960, p. 147.

11. Ibid., p. 147.

12. *The Upanishads*, Swami Prabhavananda and Frederick Manchester (trans.), Mentor Book MD 194, New American Library of World Literature, New York, 1957, p. 20, quoted by Stace, p. 118.

13. Henry Suso, *Life of Henry Suso*, T. F. Knox (trans.), chapter 54, quoted by Stace, p. 113.

14. Paul Mendes-Flohr (ed.), *Ecstatic Confessions*, collected and introduced by Martin Buber, Harper & Row, San Francisco, 1985, p. 2.

15. Ibid., p. 4.

16. *The Confessions of Saint Augustine*, Edward B. Pusey, O.D. (trans.), Washington Square Press, New York, 1962, p. 37.

17. Evelyn Underhill, *Mysticism*, New American Library, New York, 1974, p. 108.

18. Bhagavan Das (ed.), *The Essential Unity of All Religions*, Theosophical Publishing House, Wheaton, Ill., 1966, p. 263.

19. St. Teresa of Avila, *Interior Castle*, E. Allison Peers (trans. and ed.), Doubleday, Garden City, N.Y., 1961, p. 209.

20. Katharine Trevelyan, *Through Mine Own Eyes*, Holt, Rinehart and Winston, New York, 1962, pp. 120-121.

21. *Ecstatic Confessions*, p. 87.

22. *Breakthrough: Meister Eckhart's Creation Spirituality in New Translation*, introduction and commentaries by Matthew Fox, O.P., Doubleday, Garden City, N.Y., 1980, p. 65.

23. W. T. Stace, *Mysticism and Philosophy*, Jeremy P. Tarcher, Inc., Los Angeles, 1960, p. 167.

24. Lao-Tzu, *The Way of Life*, R. B. Blakney (trans.), Mentor Books, New American Library of World Literature, New York, 1955, quoted by Stace, p. 168.

25. D. T. Suzuki, *Mysticism: Christian and Buddhist*, Harper & Brothers, New York, 1927, p. 69, quoted by Stace, p. 169.

26. James Dillet Freeman, *The Story of Unity*, Unity Books, Unity Village, Mo., 1978, p. 262.

27. *Meister Eckhart*, R. H. Blakney (trans.), Harper & Brothers, New York, 1941, Sermon 24, p. 211, quoted by Stace, p. 173.

28. Henri de Lubac, S.J., *Teilhard de Chardin: The Man and His Meaning*, Rene Hague (trans.), New American Library, New York, 1965, p. 22.

29. Raynor C. Johnson, *Watcher on the Hills*, Hodder and Stoughton, London, 1959, p. 23.

30. Ibid, p. 124.

31. Abraham Isaac Kook, *The Lights of Penitence, The Moral Principles, Lights of Holiness, Essays, Letters, and Poems*, Paulist Press, New York, 1978, p. 85.

32. Aldous Huxley, *Grey Eminence*, Carroll & Graf, New York, 1941, p. 80.

33. Arthur W. Osborn, *The Axis and the Rim*, Thomas Nelson & Sons, New York, 1967, p. 107.

34. Margaret Isherwood, *The Root of the Matter*, Harper & Brothers, New York, 1954, p. 218.

35. Charles Fillmore, *Mysteries of Genesis*, Unity Books, Unity Village, Mo., 1936, p. 39.

36. Aldous Huxley, *The Perennial Philosophy*, Harper & Row, New York, 1944, p. 81.

37. Ibid., p. 178.

38. Richard Maurice Bucke, M.D., *Cosmic Consciousness*, E. P. Dutton, New York, 1901, p. 197.

39. *Breakthrough*, pp. 233, 235.

40. Ibid., p. 139.

41. Ibid., p. 327.

42. Bucke, p. 190.

43. Anne Fremantle (ed.), *The Protestant Mystics*, Little, Brown & Co., Boston, 1964, p. 48.

44. Emanuel Swedenborg, *Angelic Wisdom Concerning Divine Love and Wisdom*, Citadel Press, New York, 1965, p. 70.

45. Huxley, *The Perennial Philosophy*, pp. 181-182.

46. Charles Fillmore, *The Twelve Powers of Man*, Unity Books, Unity Village, Mo., 1930, pp. 5-6.

47. Thomas E. Witherspoon, *Myrtle Fillmore: Mother of Unity*, Unity Books, Unity Village, Mo., 1977, p. 285.

48. Huxley, *The Perennial Philosophy*, p. 229.

49. Starr Daily, *You Can Find God*, Fleming H. Revell Company, Westwood, N.J., 1963, pp. 72, 71.

50. Jae Jah Noh, *Do You See What I See?*, Theosophical Publishing House, Wheaton, Ill., 1977, p. 32.

51. Bucke, p. 10.

52. Happold, p. 135.

53. Nona Coxhead, *The Relevance of Bliss*, St. Martin's Press, New York, 1985, p. 35.

54. Evelyn Underhill, *Practical Mysticism*, E. P. Dutton, New York, 1948, p. ix.

55. Etty Hillesum, *An Interrupted Life: The Diaries of Etty Hillesum*, Washington Square Press, New York, 1981, pp. 253, 247.

CHAPTER 6

1. Paul Mendes-Flohr (ed.), *Ecstatic Confessions*, collected and introduced by Martin Buber, Harper & Row, San Francisco, 1985, p. 122.

2. Arthur W. Osborn, *The Expansion of Awareness*, Theosophical Publishing House, Wheaton, Ill., 1967, p. 244.

3. *Breakthrough: Meister Eckhart's Creation Spirituality in New Translation*, introduction and commentaries by Matthew Fox, O.P., Doubleday, Garden City, N.Y., 1980, p. 104.

4. Erwin Schroedinger, "The Mystic Vision," *Quantum Questions: Mystical Writings of the World's Great Physicists*, Ken Wilber (ed.), Shambhala, Boulder, Colo., 1984, p. 97.

5. Lawrence LeShan, *The Medium, the Mystic, and the Physicist*, Viking, New York, 1966, p. 70.

6. Ibid., p. 66.

7. Honore de Balzac, *Seraphita: A Daughter of Eve*, Gebbie Publishing Co., Philadelphia, 1899, p. 141.

8. Johannes Anker-Larsen, *With the Door Open*, Erwin and Pleasaunce von Gaisberg (trans.), Macmillan, London, 1931, quoted by Anne Fremantle, (ed.), *The Protestant Mystics*, Little, Brown & Co., Boston, 1964, pp. 311-312.

9. Loran Hurnscot, *A Prison, A Paradise*, Viking, New York, 1958, quoted by Anne Fremantle, pp. 367-368.

10. Katharine Trevelyan, *Through Mine Own Eyes*, Holt, Rinehart and Winston, New York, 1962, p. 121.

11. Ibid., pp. 219-220.

12. *Ecstatic Confessions*, p. 38.

13. Balzac, pp. 18-19.

14. Pierre Teilhard de Chardin, *The Phenomenon of Man*, Harper & Row, New York, 1959, p. 234.

15. Aldous Huxley, *The Perennial Philosophy*, Harper & Row, New York, 1944, p. 211.

16. Aldous Huxley, *Vedanta for the Western World*, Marcel Rodd Co., Hollywood, Calif., 1946, quoted by Margaret Isherwood, *The Root of the Matter*, Harper & Brothers, New York, 1954, p. 226.

CHAPTER 7

1. Raynor C. Johnson, *Watcher on the Hills*, Hodder and Stoughton, London, 1959, p. 127.

2. F. C. Happold, *Mysticism*, Penguin Books, Middlesex, England, 1970, p. 21.

3. Joel S. Goldsmith, *A Parenthesis in Eternity*, Harper & Row, New York, 1963, p. 169.

4. Ibid., p. 179.

5. Arthur W. Osborn, *The Axis and the Rim*, Thomas Nelson & Sons, New York, 1967, p. 107.

6. Goldsmith, p. 98.

7. Andrew M. Greeley, *Ecstasy: A Way of Knowing*, Prentice-Hall, Englewood Cliffs, N.J., 1974, p. 66.

8. Margaret Prescott Montague, *Twenty Minutes of Reality*, E. P. Dutton, New York, 1917, quoted by Anne Fremantle (ed.), *The Protestant Mystics*, Little, Brown & Co., Boston, 1964, p. 320.

9. Ibid., pp. 320-321.

10. Evelyn Underhill, *Mysticism*, New American Library, New York, 1974, pp. 76-77.

11. Arthur M. Abell, *Talks With Great Composers*, Psychic Book Club, London, 1955, pp. 6-7.

12. Ibid., pp. 5-6.

13. Johnson, p. 111.

14. Ibid., p. 112.

15. Happold, pp. 137-138.

16. Agnes Arber, *The Manifold and the One*, Theosophical Publishing House, Wheaton, Ill., 1967, pp. 15-16.

17. Johnson, pp. 47-48.

18. Anwar el-Sadat, *In Search of Identity: An Autobiography*, Harper & Row, New York, 1977, p. 73.

19. Ibid., pp. 76-77.

20. Ibid., pp. 85-87.

21. Paramahansa Yogananda, *Autobiography of a Yogi*, Self-Realization Fellowship, Los Angeles, 1975, p. 125.

22. Ibid., pp. 166-167.

23. Ibid., p. 168.

24. *Breakthrough: Meister Eckhart's Creation Spirituality in New Translation*, introduction and commentaries by Matthew Fox, O.P., Doubleday, Garden City, N.Y., 1980, p. 101.

25. Goldsmith, pp. 41-42.

CHAPTER 8

1. Joel S. Goldsmith, *A Parenthesis in Eternity*, Harper & Row, New York, 1963, p. 29.

2. Nona Coxhead, *The Relevance of Bliss*, St. Martin's Press, New York, 1985, pp. 63-64.

3. Goldsmith, p. 42.

4. Ibid., p. 53.

5. Ibid., pp. 354-355.

6. Aldous Huxley, *The Perennial Philosophy*, Harper & Row, New York, 1944, p. 106.

7. Anwar el-Sadat, *In Search of Identity: An Autobiography*, Harper & Row, New York, 1977, pp. 84-85.

8. Evelyn Underhill, *Mysticism*, New American Library, New York, 1974, pp. 233, 234.

9. Ibid., p. 383.

10. Ibid., p. 396.

11. Raynor C. Johnson, *Watcher on the Hills*, Hodder and Stoughton, London, 1959, p. 119.

12. Underhill, p. 402.

13. Ibid., p. 421.

14. Ibid., p. 420.

15. Ibid., p. 424.

16. Ursula King, *Towards a New Mysticism*, Seabury Press, New York, 1980, p. 101.

17. Jae Jah Noh, *Do You See What I See?*, Theosophical Publishing House, Wheaton, Ill., 1977, p. 15.

18. Bernadette Roberts, *The Experience of No-Self*, Shambhala, Boston, 1985, p. 158.

19. Sisirkumar Ghose, *Mystics as a Force for Change*, Theosophical Publishing House, Wheaton, Ill., 1981, pp. 91-92.

20. Underhill, p. 431.

21. Ibid., p. 173.

22. William James, *The Varieties of Religious Experience*, Modern Library, New York, 1936, p. 404.

23. James Dillet Freeman, *The Story of Unity*, Unity Books, Unity Village, Mo., 1987, p. 42.

24. Henry P. Van Dusen, *Dag Hammarskjöld: The Statesman and His Faith*, Harper & Row, New York, 1967, p. 110.

CHAPTER 9

1. Abraham H. Maslow, *Toward a Psychology of Being*, D. Van Nostrand Company, New York, 1962, p. 80.

2. Sisirkumar Ghose, *Mystics as a Force for Change*, Theosophical Publishing House, Wheaton, Ill., 1981, p. 57.

3. Rufus M. Jones, *The Eternal Gospel*, Macmillan, New York, 1938, p. 184.

4. Abraham H. Maslow, *Religions, Values, and Peak-Experiences*, Ohio State University Press, Columbus, 1964, p. 63.

5. Raynor C. Johnson, *Watcher on the Hills*, Hodder and Stoughton, London, 1959, p. 160.

6. J. Trevor, *My Quest for God*, London, 1897, quoted by William James, *The Varieties of Religious Experience*, Modern Library, New York, 1936, pp. 388-389.

7. Sri Aurobindo, *The Life Divine*, quoted by Ghose, p. 111.

8. Ibid., p. 112.

9. Pierre Teilhard de Chardin, *How I Believe*, Rene Hague (trans.), Harper & Row, New York, 1969, p. 44.

10. Pierre Teilhard de Chardin, *The Divine Milieu*, Harper & Row, New York, 1960, p. 146.

11. Joel S. Goldsmith, *A Parenthesis in Eternity*, Harper & Row, New York, 1963, p. 134.

12. Paul Mendes-Flohr (ed.), *Ecstatic Confessions*, collected and introduced by Martin Buber, Harper & Row,

San Francisco, 1985, pp. 133, 131, 132.

13. Margaret Isherwood, *The Root of the Matter*, Harper & Brothers, New York, 1954, pp. 211, 212.

14. Arnold Toynbee, *Christianity Among the Religions of the World*, Scribner's, New York, 1957, p. 96.

15. Evelyn Underhill, *Mysticism*, New American Library, New York, 1974, p. 96.

16. Isherwood, p. 212.

17. Toynbee, pp. 296-297.

18. Maslow, p. 19.

19. Abraham Isaac Kook, *The Lights of Penitence, The Moral Principles, Lights of Holiness, Essays, Letters and Poems*, Ben Zion Bokser (trans.), Paulist Press, New York, 1978, p. 232.

20. Ben Zion Bokser, *The Jewish Mystical Tradition*, Pilgrim Press, New York, 1981, p. 264.

21. Ursula King, *Towards a New Mysticism*, Seabury Press, New York, 1980, p. 162.

22. Louis Finkelstein (ed.), *American Spiritual Autobiographies*, Harper & Brothers, New York, 1948, pp. 114, 115.

23. Andrew M. Greeley, *Ecstasy: A Way of Knowing*, Prentice-Hall, Englewood Cliffs, N.J., 1974, p. 58.

24. John L. Hill, *The Enlightened Society*, Theosophical Publishing House, Wheaton, Ill., 1987, pp. 145, 146, 147.

25. *A Course in Miracles*, Text, vol. 1, Foundation for Inner Peace, Huntington Station, N.Y., 1975, p. 185.

26. Ghose, p. 41.

Louann Stahl *teaches courses in composition and fiction at Penn Valley Community College in Kansas City, Missouri. Her primary interest outside of teaching is metaphysics, which she sees as directly related to her volunteer work with local and national organizations that promote harmony and understanding among all peoples. She is past coordinator for the Center for World Community in Kansas City and past chairperson of UNICEF committees in Kansas City, Missouri, and Tulsa, Oklahoma. Currently she and her husband Sheldon Stahl are copresidents of the Kansas City chapter of the United Nations Association. They reside in Kansas City, Missouri, with two canine friends, Tess and Esme.*

Printed U.S.A.

45-2938-75C-12-92